Courage & Faith

Eileen Gelsomini

AuthorHouse™
1663 Liberty Drive
Bloomington, IN 47403
www.authorhouse.com
Phone: 1-800-839-8640

©2009 Eileen Gelsomini. All rights reserved.

No part of this book may be reproduced, stored in a retrieval system, or transmitted by any means without the written permission of the author.

First published by AuthorHouse 12/21/2009

ISBN: 978-1-4490-6089-3 (e)
ISBN: 978-1-4490-6092-3 (sc)

Library of Congress Control Number: 2009913390

Printed in the United States of America
Bloomington, Indiana

This book is printed on acid-free paper.

DEDICATION

To my husband John and children, Valerie, Michael and Stephanie – The greatest joy in my life.

A NOTE FROM THE AUTHOR

I wrote this book as therapy for myself. I also wrote this so that anyone who reads this and is not familiar with the military will gain some knowledge as to a fraction of what it costs both emotionally and physically for our military and their families and the price they pay for that sacrifice.

The letters and e-mails in this book are uncensored.

We as a nation do not recognize that without our military, America would not sustain. We take our military for granted and the freedom it affords us all.

This book in part is dedicated to the United States Military who unselfishly give themselves to protect this country. And for those who have given the ultimate sacrifice I honor them and their families. God Bless.

ACKNOWLEDGMENTS

To my son, Michael – For standing by your decision and not listening to me.

You showed me what true courage and patriotism is.

To my husband John – thank you for letting me lean on you both mentally and physically. You were my rock these last 4 years.

My daughter Stephanie – whose accomplishments in college may have taken a back seat many times but you not only understood, you went full throttle and graduated with honors.

My daughter Valerie and son in law Dave – For allowing me to add the footnote at the end of this book!!!

Nick – You were a "surrogate" son for John and could always be counted on to talk baseball and working out.

Lori – For being a great friend to Michael all these years.

My parents Paul and Lillian Litchfield – For your support and listening to my constant worry. Mom – thank you for your prayers.

Our family, friends and co-workers– Thank you for your countless care packages and letters to Mike.

CHAPTER ONE –
Calm before the Storm.

A young man climbs an impossible looking cliff. His footing slips a little as he stumbles and regains control of the climb. His face is beading with sweat; he has a look of determination. Will he make it you wonder? He finally made it to the top of the mountain where he stands tall and proud. Before your eyes he is transformed from an ordinary 18 year old to a proud US Marine. I turn off the Television go into the bathroom and blow my nose. No matter how many times I see that commercial… my eyes tear up. The following is the story of my son, Michael and his 4 years of service for this country in the U.S. Marine Corps. I'll take you through boot camp, two deployments to Iraq up until the time of his discharge. I am Michael's mom…and this is my story.

Let's backtrack a few years to 2000 when I wouldn't have paid any attention to that particular commercial.

Eileen Gelsomini

My son is outside and he is role playing combat action with his friend and neighbor John. They take turns being the "bad guy" shooting each other until it's time for lunch and I call them inside. Now I guess most mothers would have a talk with their child about this kind of Saturday afternoon game playing. You know guns and all. Not me, I don't give it a second thought. Just teenage kids having some fun.

I don't mind the military games that he plays on the computer either. Some kids like sports, Mike likes the military games. Little did I realize that a few short years later, those military games would be real life for my son. Real action and real death.

2003 – Senior Year High School

Michael told his father that he may want to join the Marine Corp. My husband, John informs me that it's just a phase and once he looks into it, he'll change his mind. "You know your son", he says, "he joins something and then loses interest". "He'll never go thru with this, don't worry". And meanwhile, I shouldn't mention anything to Mike about that conversation and joining the Marine Corp. Let's pretend it never happened. "Ok, I'll try" I told John. "Start seriously thinking about colleges" I plead with Mike. His father and I take Michael all over Massachusetts looking at colleges. He loves to cook. He's actually an extraordinary cook. "How about

Courage & Faith

becoming a Chef I ask him"? He gives it some thought. We visit a few Culinary Schools. Michael brings up the Marine Corps again. What about becoming an architect? "There you go" I say to Mike. You were always good at Legos. "You played with your Legos until you were what, 15"? I think I may have embarrassed him. Meanwhile, his friend, John who lived up the street had joined the Marine Corp early acceptance program with permission from his parents. What are his parents thinking I asked myself? I start to become just a little worried. His friend John has to go to PT (physical training) once a month at the recruiting station. He has to meet with his recruiter once a week either in person or over the phone. Once Mike sees this, it'll change his mind I think to myself. He'll never make that commitment. Whew! That's a relief.

One afternoon while I was cleaning Mike's room I found some literature on the Marine Corp. "Look" I say to my husband. "Now what?" "You had better have a heart to heart talk with your son" I say, in a voice becoming more and more upset. It's after 9/11 and there is talk of the United States military going to Iraq. That night my husband quietly speaks to Michael. "Whatever you do, Mike" he says, "don't sign anything unless I am with you or can look it over". Ok? "Ok dad", he promises. My husband assures me that he cannot sign anything anyway because he is not 18 yet. I feel better now knowing that my husband will talk him out of whatever ridiculous plans he has of joining the Marine Corp.

Eileen Gelsomini

Everything is going as planned. Mike has filled out some college applications, talk of joining the Marine Corp have subsided. All is well.

Mike's 18th birthday comes and goes. Thoughts of the Marine Corp have drifted out of my thoughts. While driving to work one night to pass the time, I was daydreaming about my three children. My oldest daughter was on her own, my youngest was still in High School and my only son, my middle child, I imagine getting him settled in his dorm room. Hope he doesn't drink too much like the other kids I think to myself. Maybe he'll meet a nice girl too! I'm relieved to think we dodged that bullet, the whole Military thing. God I'm glad he got over that.

It's quiet when I walk into the house that night. Too quiet. My husband waited until I took off my coat. "Sit down" he said. My heart starts to race. "I need to tell you something. " Now promise me you'll listen and not get upset." "I promise" I lied. Mike signed up and joined the Marine Corp John said.

"What"! I yelled. I didn't wait for an explanation. I burst into my son's bedroom, woke him up and began to yell. "We are going to war Mike" I yelled. "Now isn't the time to join." My husband walked in the bedroom and being the calm one in this family pointed to his signature on the contract. Four years it read. I'm not going to see my son for four years. What if the next time I see him it's in a body bag I scream. I start to lose it. Then I read the fine print at the bottom. Four years active. Four years inactive reserve. What kept me from passing out, I'll never know. I don't remember much about that night. I don't remember if my son said anything to me. I only remember thinking to myself how am I going to tell my parents that their grandson joined the military? What's going to become of him? What is he going to do for a living? Why me. Why does everyone else have a son about to go college except me? My husband explained to me later on that night that Michael was going to be a firefighter in the Marine Corp. I didn't know there was such a thing. Is that what he wants to be I ask? I find out that Michael has always been interested in becoming a firefighter. He had even e-mailed the Boston Fire Commissioner when he was 15. I thought I knew everything about my children. I was wrong.

I call the parents of my sons' friend John. Maybe they can commiserate with me and make me feel better. Misery loves company. They are amazingly calm about the whole thing. Level headed, and calm. That makes me mad.

My husband, John, told me that we have to support him in whatever he does. Deep down I know that. Doesn't every parent know that? I dread calling my parents.

When I tell them and the rest of my family and friends, they are all shocked. Can you talk him out of it they asked? Is he crazy? What is he thinking? You didn't talk to him enough when he was growing up about the importance of a college education I guess one person said to me. Now John and I did not attend college. My husband is in the construction business and I am an Esthetician. So that explains it, most people think. Like parents, like child. What can you expect? They don't say it out loud, but I know it's what they are thinking. Wrong! I feel like telling them. Look at how we've struggled I've always told my children. Well life doesn't work out the way we plan I soon realize. As the weeks pass, the comments from people get worse and worse. I feel like I have to apologize for my son's decision.

My mothers' protective instinct soon takes over. I see my son excited when he talks of what he expects to do and accomplish. He attends the new recruit meetings. Willingly.

He has a new outlook on his future. He is enthusiastic and we can't get Mike to stop talking of his recruiter and military life. If this is what my son wants I will do my best to try to understand his decision. And heaven help the person who from now on says anything negative to him or me.

"We want to meet with your recruiter" I say to Mike. "Dad and I have some questions for him", I say calmly with half a smile. On the inside, I want to scream at him for stealing my only son and potentially putting him in harms way. "Oh good, because he wants to meet with you too" Mike informs me. Yeah, sure he does I think to myself. I'm his worse nightmare.

It was a beautiful day and John and I are looking out the picture window just waiting for this "recruiter" person. Mom, please address him as Staff Sgt. Crust. "Ok, Ok, what's the big deal, can't I just call him Sgt"? I say to Mike. Staff Sgt. S.S. for short should stand for Son Stealing. I laugh to myself mainly to put me at ease. The car pulled into the driveway. It was an ordinary looking car, maybe a Ford Taurus. I don't know what I expected, a military tank? I look as the Staff Sgt got out of his vehicle. I wonder what my neighbors are thinking right now. Does anyone see this military person getting out of his car? The recruiter is young, maybe late 20's. Ok I admit, I'm nervous. Are we being interviewed? Wait a minute; he's the one that should be nervous and looking to impress me! My son introduces the Staff Sgt. Ok, that's a little weird right there. MY son is actually introducing a grown up to us. I didn't know my son knew how to do that. I see Michael looking at this Staff Sgt like he was a god. We spoke for about 1 hour. He is very honest. "Is there a chance Michael may have to go to Iraq"? I ask. "Yes", he informs us. "A very good chance". He is brutally honest and answers all of our questions. Not at all like the scene from the movie Private Benjamin where the recruiter paints a delightful picture of Military life. I hear words like, Barracks and MOS, Infantry and training. "Is he definitely going to be a firefighter in the Corp I ask"? "Yes he is" the recruiter replies. That made me feel somewhat better. He explained the entire three month intense boot camp. He handed us a video and his card. He explained that every weekend Mike will have to attend PT (Physical Training) and also community service when needed until he left for boot camp.

"So he has not actually "joined" the Marine Corp yet"? I asked. No, the recruiter explains, he can still bail out up until he takes the final swearing in oath in Boston before he boards the bus to the airport. Ah ha....I say almost out loud. There is still a chance he won't continue with this. I keep that thought to myself. I tuck it safely away, hidden and pull it out at different times during the summer up until August.

We throw a "Graduation/Good Bye party for Mike during the summer. Around 70 of our family and friends were there. It was bittersweet. One of his gifts from John's cousin was a money clip of St. Michael with a prayer on it. (The significance of this gift will appear in another chapter).

CHAPTER TWO
August 2003 – Marine Corp Boot camp – Parris Island.

The whole month of July flew by. This was the last time I would see my son on a daily basis for the next four years. No one spoke about it in our family. We go on with our life as usual. I cry in private times. Aside from my husband, no one understands. I do not know any other military family.

August 3rd, 2003. D-Day.

Michael is all packed, ready and waiting to leave our home. He is allowed the clothes on his back and $10.00. Try to imagine that you are sending your child away for four years with almost nothing. My husband and I look out the window watching for Staff Sgt Crusts' car. "Here he comes" my husband said. We watch the car slowly go by our house down the street to his childhood friends' house, John to pick him up as well. "At least he is going to Parris Island with a friend" I say to John for comfort. (After boot camp he won't see John for another 4 years) I'm still silently holding back the thought that he may change his mind. I look over at my son. Judging by his face, he will not. He looked nervous, but determined. The car pulled into the driveway. I want to wake up and think this is a bad dream. John and I walk Michael outside to the car. I still can't believe this is happening. His friend John is smiling in the back seat. We laugh nervously at him and wave. At least he has a buddy with him we say. We hug and kiss our son good-bye as he got into the back seat with his friend. This whole process takes no longer than 10 minutes. Like ripping off a band aid; the quicker, the less pain. We stand there, my husband and me as the recruiter backed out and we wave and smile. My son is half smiling. His friend has the biggest grin on his face. Two young men who don't have a clue as to what they are in for. We stand in the driveway, I turn and fall into my husbands arms and cry. I had no idea what the next four years would bring. John and I watch until we can no longer see the recruiter's vehicle. We walk into the house silently. Suddenly the house seemed so quiet. Days later, I find myself looking into Mike's room on a daily basis trying to remember him lying on his bed with his earphones on.

Courage & Faith

A few days passed and we were told that we would receive a phone call from Michael saying that he arrived safely at Parris Island. And that is literally what Mike said. Nothing more. A quick, Hi Mom, can't talk, I've arrived safe, got to go. Bye. That was the last time I heard my son's voice for the next three months. Every day at work I signed onto the website for Marine parents at Parris Island to follow the day to day activities of their sons and daughters at boot camp. I printed out the event calendar and hung it on my cubicle wall. At night, I went from work to school to study for my Estheticians license. It kept me busy which was a Godsend. One night while driving home I heard on the news that President Bush was launching his "Shock and Awe campaign. We had officially gone to war. I remember making the sign of the cross in the car. The next day, my co-workers reassured me that the "war" would be over in about three months. I was not to worry about my son. Of course they knew what they were talking about. Most of my co-workers were ex-military themselves and they knew more about such things than I did. Still, something nagged at me. I continued waiting for a letter from my son. Here is his first letter from Parris Island.

Hi Mom, Dad, Val Steph, I miss you all so much. I am really homesick right now and this is really hard to deal with. I wish that I was home right now with you guys. I really want to be with all of you. It is only Thursday the 3rd *day that we have been here and we are still in the receiving process. We are in a temp. squad bay till Sat. when we move It is tough right now. But when we meet our real DI's it will get ten times more intense. It is really hard adjusting so far to the routine but it is getting better. My platoon is pretty cool. We have some immature people though that will get us in trouble very soon. We found out 3rd Battalion Indian Company is the hardest of all and concentrates on PT. I am somewhat excited to move on. It is motivating to see platoons further in training and wanting to be like them, but for now we have major discipline problems .Our receiving DI is tough but he is cool. We have no way of mailing letters till we get to our permanent squad bay. When we have free time, we'll get to hit the rack early because we were good today. Today was really hard because it was family day and it made me really wanna see you all. You guys are all I can think about. I really want to be home right now, but at the same time I really wanna finish training. I just need more motivation because I want to be home more. I miss you all so much. I don't care about anything else but seeing you guys. I don't know when I can send this so it might be late. Please write but not every day cause it'll be hard to find time to read them and to write back. Our platoon number is 3091. I'm gonna hit the rack now we haven't gotten much sleep. I love you all so much. Please send only letters I love you. Mike*

My eyes started to fill up when I read this to my husband over the phone. I admit I wanted to fly down there and take him home. I knew of course I couldn't. "Hit the rack". What the heck is it that he is sleeping on?" Does he have a pillow? Do they give him enough blankets? He'll make some friends my husband assured me and this is what he wanted, remember?

Excerpts from Mike's second boot camp letter

Hey mom, dad, Val, Steph. I haven't heard from you guys in about a week. When I said cut back on the mail, I take it back, write whenever you can. Is everything Ok at home? Not much new is really going on. I'm eating good. I eat like 2 things of fruit with every meal and our Senior DI has us have one glass of milk with every meal.

(Fruit and Milk Huh. Why I couldn't even get him to do that. Maybe the DI is really nice, I think, kind of like a mother figure) He goes on...

I can't wait for that car ride home so we can have all that time to catch up on stuff because I'm missing so much. Have a lot of time to think about stuff. I realized I really look up to you Mom and Dad. Like being able to do all you do and keep going. You guys put up with so much and have worked so hard to get where you at now. Hope to hear from you soon. Love you mom, love you dad, love you Val love you steph. Love mike.

Eileen Gelsomini

What's happening here? What happened to my son? The kid with the Mohawk green hair, baggy pants, and "I'll get to it later" attitude? With every letter, brings more surprises.

Hello my family

These past few days the weather has been really cool and windy. Today we had 80 lbs of gear and had to jump off a tower into the pool. Half the platoon failed. We have pictures tomorrow. I'm excited for that. I hope I look good. I am dying to get out to the rifle range. I got some time to look at all your letters. I almost teared up a little. Well I did, but not cry. I've only cried in the Hotel when I was on the phone with you guys. I'm still not over home sick. I took my family for granted and now I regret not spending as much time with you all as I could have. I really love you all so much. I realize how much family is important to me. I pray for you guys in church every Sunday. Ok, I gotta stop now, I'll pick up later.

I wonder if I'll have any more tears left at the end of boot camp. The poor thing cried in the Hotel the night before he left Boston to Boot Camp. I can't bear this anymore. It moves me every time I re-read how much his loves and misses us. And Church? What's this, he's going to church down there? That I had to tell to my mother!

The weeks ahead Mike shared many more experiences with us through his letters. Two things were very apparent.

One, he missed us terribly. Two, he was afraid he would be dropped at the rifle qualifications. That is where most of the recruits get dropped. I for one wasn't that worried about it. I say that as I look into his bedroom and see all the BB Holes he put in his wall with accuracy! Still we prayed for him and that he would pass everything and fail nothing. The countdown was October 31st – Graduation.

Hey what's up? Today is Monday the first day on the range. I actually did pretty Damn good. When I was on the 500 yard line which is pretty damn far shooting on targets called B-Modified (targets of men life-size) I was shooting dead center and the Sr DI saw and he was like good Dam shooting Gelsomini... I have been thinking a lot. I have the best parents like on everything, but I mainly am talking about like work ethic and how you raised me. You guys raised me by example; you both busted your asses so hard to get to where you are. When you guys have something to get done you do it. You don't' complain you just get it done. Like dad, every time I've been to work with you, you are just constantly busting your ass and when I see you doing projects at work or home you do what ever it takes. Mom you put up with so much at work and still keep with it. You're now working 2 jobs and going for shit you wanna do and did what it takes to get there. I try to keep all that with me when I'm feeling lazy and don't wanna do stuff, but I think of you two and what you taught me and how I wanna model myself after you guys. It's hard to explain but in my mind and heart it's clear. I want to have your guy's work ethic and stuff. You are great parents just so you know. You raised me right and taught me so much about life and most of it was by example. You can tell you're parents raised you right. I love you guys thank you so much. Love you mom and dad, love mike. Love you Val and Steph. Write me girls.

Ok, I can die now. That's how I felt after reading that letter and all of his letters. I wanted to bring that to work and show everyone. Of course I didn't. I don't think I will ever be as proud of my son as the moment I read that letter.

Rifle qualification day was here. My mind wasn't on my work; it wasn't on my studies at night. I prayed Mike would pass this rifle qualification test. Since we cannot speak with Mike, all we could do was to wait for a letter. Finally we received his letter.

Hey family, I don't have much time to write. Friday we had Qual. Day with the range. I shot Expert, the highest you can get and I also shot the highest point wise in my platoon, so I get to wear the expert badge.

I immediately called John. I guess I can only explain it this way. It would be like your child getting a 1600 on the SAT's. I know that people don't understand how proud we were when I tell them that my son took a rifle and shot it at a distance of 5 football fields away and hit a target of a man dead center. He just wanted to pass and he excelled and was the best in his platoon! Ok I admit it, I finally crossed over. I'm officially a Marine Mom. I realize that I no longer yearn to help my son unpack his bags in his college dorm. That I don't dream he'll meet his "future wife" at some college dance. I proudly display Marine Mom bumper stickers on my car. Quite a few of them. I wear Marine pins at work on my shirt. We hung an American flag on the flagpole attached to the house. We hung a Marine Corp flag on the other side of the door. We are officially a Marine Corp Family.

Every afternoon after the mailman came to our home, I run out to get the mail. I think he must know that I have a son in the Marine Corp. He must see the letters and of course he sees the American flag flying as well as the Marine Corp Flag.

October is finally here. Countdown is started.

The Crucible –

The crucible is a 52 hour exercise in mental and physical discipline. The recruits go thru various stages with only about 8 hours of sleep during that entire period. It is the last obstacle they must overcome. They can only pass this by teamwork, courage, and commitment. When we didn't hear from him, we knew he has passed this last test. Our son was coming home!

Eileen Gelsomini

Excerpts from his last letter from Boot camp.

Hey Family, I'm so damn excited. I get to come home in only 19 days. I can't wait to see you on family day in my uniform and stuff. I'll be in my service charlies green trousers, short sleeve khaki shirt with badges and my green flat cover. I wanna see your faces and give each of you huge ass hugs. I have so much to catch up on with all of you and I'm sure you have tons of questions for me. I can't wait for that long ass car drive home. I'm looking forward to all that time with my great family. Can I have front seat for a little Mom? I think this might be one of my last letters. I can't wait to come home and sit down at dinner with you guys and relax or sit in the living room and talk. I hope you guys can keep up with me at dinner. You will have to force me to spread my feet and take my left hand off my knee and force me to eat slowly. You gotta stock up on food when I come back. But anyways, mom and dad, hang in there I love you two so much and everything you've ever done for me. I really appreciate it all now even if I didn't seem like it at the time. Thank you. I love you Val , Steph. Thank you for being great sisters you're the best. Can't wait to hang out with you two. Thank you for writing me, thank you I love you two so much. Tell Chucky I'm coming home soon. (Chucky is our dog) I love you all, best family ever, your son, brother – Mike. Ps have a safe journey down please.

Parris Island Graduation.

My parents were driving up from Florida to meet us at the Hotel in South Carolina.

My oldest daughter Valerie was driving down with us. My youngest daughter Stephanie was taking the SAT's. and couldn't make it.

We left early in the morning. There was a huge rainstorm from Massachusetts all the way thru Maryland. A hurricane wouldn't have stopped us though. We couldn't get there fast enough. We stopped just long enough to stretch our legs, eat and go to the restroom.

Finally we made it down. I was in the same state as my son! I never thought this day would come.

Family day is Thursday, the day before graduation. This is the day you get to actually hug your son, and speak to him. They have an assembly first and there is a band playing and also a ceremony afterwards. This takes quite a few hours. We passed the time until it started with a narrated bus ride around Parris Island. We watched the newer recruits march around the camp. American flags were everywhere. My 74 year old mother who is from the WWII Greatest Generation was so moved by this entire experience, she teared up. If you weren't patriotic before, you certainly were when you left Parris Island. At quiet moments throughout the bus ride I felt ashamed at my outburst to my son the day he said he joined. I felt honored to be among all these young men and women at

Eileen Gelsomini

Parris Island. I wanted to say to anyone who would listen to me from now on, Oh your son is a doctor, lawyer, fill in the blank...well my son is a United States Marine!

The ceremony started at 1pm. We were in our seats at ll: 30am. No one else was seated in the bleachers but us. I was going to be the first one to jump over the roping they had in front of the bleachers when it was over. Heaven help the person that tried to position themselves in front of me. I was going to be first.

The recruits came out on the parade deck. They are still referred to as recruits until they receive their Eagle Globe and Anchor Pin at Graduation the next day. We watched them march around, sing, and assemble. How orderly they all looked. How straight they stood. My husband spotted my son going by the bleachers with his fellow recruits. John ran over to him hopping two bleachers at a time. Arthritic hips? What arthritic hips! Nothing could keep him from running to catch a glimpse of his son. However, the recruits cannot make eye contact or speak with anyone. I think we knew this, but didn't think they really meant it. They did. Michael ignored my husband. He looked so young, and he dropped about 30 pounds. His face looked drawn and tired.

When the Family Day Ceremony was over and the announcer said "dismissed", you guessed it, I was the first one on that parade deck. We ran over to Michael and hugged him so tight. It wasn't quite as emotional for my son or so it seemed. I was a little taken back by this. Probably nerves and just plain tiredness I thought. After all he just had a hell of a week with the crucible. We looked for a spot to have lunch. As he was walking with my husband, I walked behind and noticed how efficient he walked. Head held high, back ramrod straight. What had they done to my son? We found a spot to eat and things were kind of quiet. This was an adjustment for him as well as for us. How were we to address him, son, Mike, recruit? He quietly told us that he really couldn't do that much hugging, and smiling. We saw his DI but Mike told us not to go over and say hello. Ok, we promised we wouldn't. We made some small talk thru dinner. After dinner we went to the store on base. We purchase about $300.00 worth of Marine Corp Logo clothing. This would officially become our wardrobe. For the next four years, my husband would only wear T shirts with the Marine Corp logo on it. 7pm rolled around and it was time to take Mike back to his barracks. Michael informed us that he could not be a minute late. We hated to leave, but graduation was tomorrow. Tomorrow we'd get our son back.

Graduation Day - Parris Island.

His name was in the graduation pamphlet as highest shooter in his platoon. We were so proud. Graduation was shorter than I thought, just over an hour. In one hour he was ours. When they played the song, "Proud To Be

An American", I don't think there was a dry eye in the stadium. This was by far the most moving experience I have ever witnessed. Very patriotic. When it was over, we said good-bye to my parents and we got into our car for the long ride home to Massachusetts. Mike sat in the front as promised by me.

He complained that his uniform was so tight and restricting.

We asked him if he wanted to change into his civilian clothes. He did not. As uncomfortable as he was in his uniform, he was proud and wore it until we reached the hotel in Maryland. We broke for dinner later that night. It was strange to see him in his uniform going into a restaurant. Yes Ma'am and thank you Ma'am were how he addressed the waitress.

My husband and I looked at each other every time he did or said something out of character. This clearly wasn't the same person who left our home three months prior.

Our son was now a U.S. Marine. We couldn't have been prouder.

CHAPTER THREE
Introduction to Military Life

During Mike's official 21 days of leave after boot camp, Mike spent his days catching up with friends and family. It was so good to finally have him home. I tried to "fatten" him up with home cooked meals. It seemed to me like he was away at summer camp. This is what I told myself. I guess I am still somewhat in denial. I don't think about him leaving again, and this time not knowing when I will see him. After his leave is up, he will be heading out to North Carolina for infantry training. My husband assures me that every Marine needs to learn this. Not to worry. Every Marine is an Infantry Marine first and his MOS comes second. This infantry training will last three weeks. Mike is actually looking forward to this. He loves guns, rifles, anything artillery. After the three weeks he'll be heading down to Florida to wait until a spot opens up at the Firefighter Academy in Texas.

"Look at all the places he is seeing right now and all the new experiences he will have", John tells me. "Look at all the people he'll meet". I guess this is supposed to make me feel better as the time approaches for him to leave again. I don't realize at the time, that these next four years will be nothing more than a series of goodbyes and fleeting glances of my son. Deep down, though, I know. But denial will be my only saving grace and something that I'll get pretty good at for survival purposes. I packed up all of Mike's belongings in his room along with all of his gifts he received at his graduation-good-bye party, put them in two boxes and sealed them. I placed them up in the attic. I left his bed, nightstand and TV in his room. He wouldn't need his civilian clothes for a while. I did this without a tear. My denial kicking in full force.

Infantry Training.

Time once again for my son to leave us. He is reporting to "official duty" and so he must wear his Marine Corp uniform. It is morning and he is stressing out because the uniform creases must be just so. He needs to hold his hat the correct way when not on his head. His pins must be exactly in the correct position on his uniform. The whole process to get dressed takes an hour. Mike asks me to look at him head on and see if his hat is exactly in the middle. I assure him it is and don't know what the fuss is all about. I realize that this is important though and so I make sure everything is the way it should be when he asks me. John and I take him to Logan Airport. His father and I sit there with him and we don't talk much. Mike is nervous. He is traveling by himself to an unfamiliar place. He has to take a taxi. Things he has never done before. "It's not like you are going to a hotel Mom", he explains. "You have to be there at an exact time". "I don't know where I'm going or who to see and people in the Marine Corp aren't helpful'. I look at this 18 year old and suddenly I see my son at 5 years old going on the school bus for the first time. My parents try to reassure me that he'll be fine. "18 year olds go away to college all the time" they say. Yes, but they have orientation at colleges, counselors at college, dorm room monitors at college, dances at college and most important people who care at colleges. Mike was on his own. John assured me again, that this will make him grow up a heck of a lot sooner than most kids his age.

We waited a while until we finally heard from him a few days later. Most of the time he was enthusiastic. Getting there wasn't easy. Reporting to Official Duty wasn't a piece of cake either. His barracks weren't ready and his questions weren't answered. And so he did what Marine's do best. He waited.

And when all else fails, improvise. "If he can get through this, John tells me, he can get through anything". We would end up using this line many times throughout his 4 years.

For the most part, Infantry training was good. He enjoyed shooting and the "war games" they played. I think back to Mike at 14 playing "war games" with his friend. Little did I know this is what he would be actually doing a few years later in training. And soon afterwards …for real.

CHAPTER FOUR
Firefighter Academy-Goodfellow Airforce Base, Texas

Florida

His infantry training was complete. Next move was on to Florida. There he would wait until he was told to leave to Texas for Firefighter Academy. He was supposed to be in Florida for about 6 weeks. It ended up being more like 2 months. December was fast approaching. We wondered if he would be able to get leave to come home for Christmas.

He gave us the word that they were allowing him leave time for the Holidays. But only about 6 days. It was going to be a Merry Christmas after all! I decorated the house, and suddenly the Holidays were going to be great. Mike was coming home. We picked him up at the airport. Christmas came and went way too fast. We made the rounds of going to relatives houses to say hello (and goodbye).

In the meantime, we kept our eye on the war in Iraq. It wasn't over, not by a long shot. It had intensified. Soldiers and Marines were dying every week. Things were not getting better. We asked Mike if he thought there may be a chance that he may have to go over to Iraq. He said he didn't know. They do not tell them anything. I remember saying to myself that he is just a "beginner Marine" and that they have a whole lot of other more experienced older Marines to choose from to go over to Iraq. I don't know if my husband thought I was crazy or if he wanted to believe that himself. But he didn't correct me. He just didn't saying anything.

We heard from Mike a few times a week during this intense Firefighter Training Academy. Michael loved it. Plain and simple. Every time he called he couldn't get the words out fast enough to explain to us what he did that day. This is what he was truly meant to do. What a great thing it is for a person at the age of 18 to know what he wants to do with his life. I guess you would say it is a "calling". Much like someone wanting to be a priest, a teacher or a doctor. Those professions aren't for everyone. Either is becoming a firefighter. There were three girls in his class. Only one made it through the academy. Without much notice he called and said he was graduating from Fire Academy. John and I wished we could have been there. We told him how proud we were of him. Something that would be said a million times over during these next four years.

He had made a lot of good friends at the Academy. One of those friends, Stanton was to become his best friend in the Marine Corp.

Life went on as usual at the Gelsomini household. John and I started planning a vacation like we normally do for the springtime. We chose to go on a cruise and take our two daughters with us. All was going well. Our daughter, Valerie was dating a nice young man, Dave, which my husband had introduced to her only a few short months ago. They became inseparable. Stephanie, our other daughter was in her sophomore year at college also dating a nice young man for quite a few years. She was living at college with her best friend and a few other girls. Michael came home after Fire Academy Training for about 10 days. He was going to be stationed at Miramar Air Base out in San Diego, California. What a place to be stationed. Palm trees, warm weather, and sunshine. In a way we acted as if he was going to college or some kind of camp for four years. We didn't speak of the war that was going on in Iraq. No one wanted to bring up that subject. If Michael knew what was to come, he didn't say anything to us.

Michael came home for a few days after firefighter academy. Our time together was precious and John and Mike went fishing, went to the gun range and spent some quality time together as father and son. I also went with them. Not that going to shoot a gun was my thing, but I would have done anything so long as it was spent with Michael. We had fun.

The time came for Michael to report to his duty station at Miramar. He was nervous as he always is with something new. New place, new rules, housing, etc. You never know in the Corp if you will report to someone decent and fair or to someone who is miserable and who takes it out on his Corporals. Because he is to report to a new duty station Michael needs to wear his uniform. He spends an hour making sure everything is straight and in place like he did before. I use the lint roller to make sure his uniform is spotless. It looked ok to me, but ok does not "fly" in the Marine Corp. You have to look perfect. No one is saying anything that morning. We eat in silence. Mike's training days are basically over and this is his official duty station. I felt "safe" before knowing that Mike still had some training to do. Michael knows that there is a good chance that he will be going off to Iraq shortly but doesn't mention that fact more than once to us.

John and I drove him to Logan Airport. We've learned that these goodbyes are awkward, emotional and extremely difficult. Because of 9/11 we are not allowed passed the security gate to wait with Michael. We went with him to the counter to get his tickets and pass in his luggage. I explain to the ticket agent behind the counter

Courage & Faith

our situation with our son going off to Iraq. I ask him if we could please wait with him in the waiting area. There has got to be a special kind of pass for this or something someone can do for us" I plead with this man. He looked unimpressed and bored. "Nothing I can do Ma'am" he said". I ask again, beg is more like it. He just shakes his head. I am emotional now and my eyes fill up. I pray someday that he has a son who is in the Military and he has precious few moments with him. I know Mike wanted us with him although he would never say it. John ushers us away from the counter and we wait on the sideline until the very last moment before Mike has to walk thru that security line. I notice that the ticket agent behind the counter left and must have went on his break. I see a women replace him. I know I can get to her. She is an older woman who looked like she may be a mother. Don't ask me how I know this, but I do. John looked at me when I told him I'll be right back. He had that look that said, don't bother. I don't give up that easily. I approach the women and with tears in my eyes explain our situation. I tell her he is my only son going to Iraq and we'd like to be with him until he leaves on the plane and wait with him. I guess I got to her because she told me to wait a minute and then came back with two special passes that would allow us the privilege of getting passed security and into that waiting room! I turn around and approach John with the best gift anyone has given me. More time with my son.

Eileen Gelsomini

So there we sit patiently waiting for his seat row to be called to board the plane. I do notice something odd with my son's behavior. Although I can't pinpoint it, it looked to me like he is off in a distance. He looked pale. John got up from his seat and said he'll be right back; he is going to the men's room. No sooner does my husband leave, Michael turned to me and said' "Mom, I can't do it, I can't go. I guess my mouth dropped open, and I looked in disbelief at what I am hearing. "What do you mean, you're not going?" "Mike, you have to go, you'll get court-martialed". I hold his hand. He grips back with the firmest grip I've ever felt. Like he wasn't going to ever let go. I am on the verge of tears. I look around in desperation to find John. No sign of him yet. I look around to see if anyone is witnessing this. Everyone seems to be keeping to themselves. Involved in their own little world. Michael said it again to me. I suggest with get up and walk. He held my hand the entire time. I suddenly feel like I am holding the hand of my 5 years old son and bringing him to Kindergarten. He starts to feel dizzy and we sit down again. He kept repeating it over and over again. I'm not going". Now I'm panicked. Really panicked. The airlines started the boarding process. They are calling out rows for boarding. I see John, thank God. I went over to John and explain what is happening. We are both seated next to Mike now. We tell him, we are going to visit him in San Diego before he left for Iraq if he should go that Fall. We tell him not to worry, we love him and we are so proud of him. None of this seems to matter though. We gently escort him back to the area where we were seated for his plane. This whole scenario is surreal to me. Here I am his mother forcing him on a plane and to a strange place where he knows no one and probably going to fight in a war in a few months. After a few minutes with John he seemed Ok. We are hugging him and now we are all crying. I don't realize it, but everyone in the seating area is looking at us. Two distraught parents hugging their only son in a Military uniform. Everyone knew what we were doing and where he was going. They call his row number. We stand up and cry and hug each other. One by one, at least 70 percent of those people in the waiting area with us approach us and shake our son's hand and wish him well. That made me cry even harder. Michael gathers his composer now and thanked every one of them. We do as well. We literally hang on to Michael until he hands in his ticket to the women. We watch him walk down that corridor onto the plane. John and I cry all the way through the airport, all the way to our car.

We are on the Massachusetts Turnpike heading home stuck in traffic. Suddenly John received a text message on his cell phone. It's from Michael. It says simply. "I love you". Just when I don't think I have any more tears left.

I'm beginning to realize that the next four years of my life are going to be a series of "goodbyes" with Mike. I hate it. I hate it that my life has to be this way. I ask God to watch over Michael.

CHAPTER 5
Worry and Wait

Springtime - 2004

Because Michael's MOS is Firefighter/Airwing support, he is assigned to the flightline at Miramar Air Base. He calls frequently; almost every day as a matter of fact. He is starting to get used to his daily schedule. Some days are long and boring. Sometimes he calls us because they had an emergency on the airfield they had to respond to.

He is either in a good mood or bad mood. There is no in between with Mike. Sometimes there are drills, or PT (Physical Training) or they have inspection for their rooms. He is with his good friend, Stanton. They seem to have fun and he calls frequently when they are together on their free time.

Courage & Faith

I have started working at my new career as an Esthetician. I love the job, I love the people. On occasion family and friends bring up the possibility of Michael going to Iraq. Our answer is always the same. We don't know. We don't think so. He's brand new to the Marine Corp and they have plenty of other Marines that are more experienced to go over I tell them. How naïve was I? During one of Michael's phone calls he gave us the heads up that he may indeed be deployed to Iraq. He will not know for sure until about June. And if he does go over it won't be until August. I don't want to hear it. I pray constantly for this not to be true. I don't mention it to anyone other than my immediate family. I have myself believing that this will never happen. Michael has a tendency to jump to conclusions I tell my husband. We don't bring up this subject again. Not to anyone, not to each other.

Summer is fast approaching and so is our cruise! I can't wait. It'll take my mind off of everything. I feel a little sad however that only two of my children will be with us. Michael called us one night to let us know that he will know by June 22 give or take three days if he is scheduled to go over to Iraq. "What timing" I say to John. Right before our cruise, I have to go on vacation knowing that my son is going to war. John reassures me that it probably won't happen. How will I ever enjoy myself I wonder? I have been praying for some time now. I know in my heart that God will answer my prayers. There is no way Michael is going over. No way. The thought is so awful that I put it out of my head entirely. It is amazing what the mind can do if you concentrate hard enough. I am uneasy that whole third week in June. I mention this to my family but I feel they really can't understand. I can't blame them. I secretly curse my son. I am desperate now as only a mother can be. Why in heavens name couldn't he go to college like the rest of the kids? I feel guilty thinking this way. My son's life is at stake and so I forgive myself. I go over and over again in my mind what I could have done differently. What I didn't say, what I could have said. I can't find a single thing that comes to mind. It's not going to happen. It's not. I pray like I have never done before that entire week.

We eat suppers quietly. No one wants to speak the unspeakable. The subject is not brought up. I have faith. He will not be called to go. Period.

Thursday, June 21st.

It is morning and I am schedule to work at noontime. I need to go into the attic and get down the suitcases for our trip. I wish Michael would call and just let us know he is not going. That would be so great I think to myself. I can go on this vacation knowing that piece of information. I have faith in my religion and God. I believe in the power of prayer. And boy have I prayed! I ask God to give me a "sign" to let me know the answer. Why hasn't he called yet? I am impatient and annoyed at the Marine Corp. I open the attic door and pull down the ladder. We don't have much in the attic and everything is in boxes. I look at the two boxes that are filled with Michael's things. One for his clothes, the other contains various other items, some of which were what he received as gifts the summer of his going away party. I can't look at them anymore and continue to take the suitcases down which are on the opposite side of the boxes. One by one, I take them down to the hallway via the ladder. I push up the ladder and close the door in the ceiling. I take the suitcases and put two in my daughters' bedroom and two in ours. Then I finished packing my suitcase and go out into the hallway to the kitchen.

I notice something on the floor. A metal object. I didn't see that before I went into the attic or any other time during the day. I didn't hear anything drop to the floor either when I went into the attic for the suitcases. I walk over to it to see what it was.

When I saw what it was, chills ran up my arm. There on the floor was the St. Michaels money clip that he received at his going away party. It was fairly heavy being made of metal. Funny how I didn't hear it drop. Even stranger was the fact that the boxes were all sealed. How on earth did this thing get out of the box and drop to the floor? Without me seeing or hearing it drop either? I immediately thought of my prayers to God and the "sign" that I had asked from him. This was it I thought! This was the sign. God is telling me not to worry, that Michael is not going over to Iraq. St. Michael protected him. I still can't believe what happened. Now someone else would probably dismiss that as just a coincidence or nothing at all. Not me. I truly believe that this was "the sign" I was waiting for. It is like a giant weight lifted off of my shoulders. I can breath!

Later that day I head off to work. It was the first day of summer. Everyone at the Spa was in a good mood. The warm weather is coming. People are talking of vacations, etc. I am fairly new there and just getting acquainted with my co-workers. We are friendly, but not "friends" just yet. I have a busy schedule and get started with my night.

Halfway through the night the front desk has a message for me. Call your husband it said.

I start to panic just a little. John never calls me. Not at any job I've had. Maybe its good news. Yes, that's it.

He knows how I've been so worried lately. I went into the other room to call John. I am alone when I call him. "John, hi, what's up"? His voice is shaky. He got right to the point. Mike just called. He is being deployed to Iraq. He is going to war.

The room started to spin. I felt blackness closing around me. I squat down to the floor because I feel like I am going to pass out. Noooo, I scream. No. No. No. Oh my God, Oh my God. John is crying over the phone. He told me he has called my parents who in turn cry as well. "When"? I ask. "Around August", John informs me. This is my son's death sentence. This can't be happening. I hang up the phone and call my sister in law, Sandra. I call my brother, Paul. I want someone to help me. Help me how, I don't know. Just help me. I went into my esthetician room and cried uncontrollably. The spa manager hugged me and one of the massage therapist hugs me as well. I can't leave; I still have two more clients. How in God's name am I going to service my clients now? Somehow I get through the night.

I drive home in tears. When I enter my house, I walk over to my husband and we hug each other and cry. Life can't get any worse than right now. We both don't know what to do. There is nothing we can do to reassure each other. We finally go to bed where we have a restless sleep. I toss and turn all night. I've only had my son for 18 years I think to myself.

Eileen Gelsomini

The following morning I sit all alone with my thoughts on our couch. God has betrayed me. Why did he send a "sign" that Mike wouldn't go when it's not true. I sit silently for hours that next day before going to work. I can't seem to focus on anything. I keep going back to that St. Michaels money clip. I prayed to God for some kind of answer. I am so mentally exhausted that I take a nap before going to work. When I wake up, it is suddenly crystal clear to me now. That indeed was a sign. That was a sign from God telling me that Michael was going over to Iraq, but that he was going to be Ok. He was going to be Ok. I knew to give that St. Michaels clip to my son to take with him. He was going to be Ok because St. Michael was going to take care of him and watch over him. God was telling me he is going over, but not to worry, he will come back. My son will come back to us.

So that was my sign. Michael was going to war, but he would be all right. I had to rely on my faith. I had to believe. I make a pact with God. I will sacrifice something if he would bring Michael back to me safely. If I give up ice-cream for the entire deployment, then he will bring Mike home safe. I know this may sound weird to some people, but I needed to believe that that would make a difference. God will take my sacrifice seriously and do this. And from that point on, all I bought was "frozen yogurt".

I couldn't go cold turkey.

Courage & Faith

We left on our cruise. We all had heavy hearts. I don't think it really sank in yet as far as my daughters' were concerned. Maybe that was for the best. Two of us in the house worried to death is all we need.

My mind goes back to the 1970's. The end of the Vietnam War was approaching and I was a teenager. My oldest brother received his draft card in the mail. I vaguely remember some whispered conversations of concern among my parents. I may have worried a little then, but being only 13, it was short lived. I had things to do, friends to see. It may be different now. My girls are older, almost 18 and 23. John and I talk about it more openly as well. The real dangers. I feel they should know.

During those 7 days on the cruise, I pretend to be "happy". I have to smile for the sake of my two daughters, and other people we meet on the cruise. I don't want to be on this cruise ship. I just want to be home. I want to quit work, stay home and curl up in my bed and sleep for the next year. The only thing that keeps me going are my girls and my husband. He seems to be holding up better than me. He's the optimist in the family. I'm the" glass is not only half empty, it's cracked as well".

When I return to work, my co-workers ask me how my vacation was. No one mentions my son. I'm not sure if this is on purpose so as not to bring the subject up for fear of upsetting me, or the concept is so far from reality from their world, they don't even think about it. It's happening "over there" and their lives go on as usual. I try to go on as usual myself. I don't bring my "problems" to work, although I think this counts as more than just a problem. It's life altering.

It is different where my husband works. I'll learn soon enough through these next 4 years that men react different to war than women. I'm not sure if they truly respect the military or are simply more informed. Whatever the case, the reactions he gets almost daily are much different than my own.

We go about business are usually during this summer of 2004. We don't mention the war too much that rages on. We don't speak of Michael going to Iraq in August. What we do however, is watch about 4 or 5 hours of news a day. We need to do this. We never used to watch much news. But it's different now. We want to find out how many troops died that day, as well as what is going on over in Iraq. I try to explain to people that it would be like having someone you loved work at the twin towers the day the planes flew into them and watching it all through the day to see if you find out if your loved one is still in there or made it out. This is the only way I can explain it. We soon find out that no one else seems that concerned. The only news they are exposed to are snippets here and there from their local news channel mostly about the deaths. The local channels don't go into the complex reasons of the war. This sad reality I'll soon find out is the very reason most women and some men

Courage & Faith

we know, spout off only negative views or completely have their facts incorrect. John and I tune in to every station for many months. We settle on one station in particular that reports all sides and views on this very controversial war. Fox cable news we find out is the only station that will give different opinions from both sides. We settle on this news station from now on.

Before this war started, sadly John and I never paid much attention to anything in politics. We did not vote, we made fun of people that stood on the side of the road during election time holding up signs for their candidates and said something to the fact that they had nothing else better to do. Do they really think those signs will make a difference?

How could we know that one day, two years from now, John would be holding up a sign of his own.

CHAPTER 6
Pre Iraq

Michael is allowed leave before his deployment to Iraq. John and I decide to go out to San Diego where he is stationed to spend some time with him. I have never been out to the west coast before. San Diego is beautiful. I'm glad my son is out here if he has to be stationed anywhere, this is great. After we are settled into our hotel room, we meet Michael in the parking lot. Michael took us on base. The rules are strict and Michael seems very serious about them. We all need to be buckled in our seatbelts. Something John and I never do even though Massachusetts has the "click it or ticket" slogan. We approach the guard gateway entrance to his base. I see the MP's (military police) at the guard house standing there looking very imposing with their guns and military like stance. I don't want to make eye contact. I'm not sure why not

Courage & Faith

either. As we slow down to stop, we show our licenses, and my son shows his ID. They wave us on. Whew, we made it in. I look around us. The base is huge. I see military stores, I see where they grocery shop, there is a bank, a movie theater. Michael took us to the flight line where he waits at "hotspots". (Place to wait for planes and helicopters to come in). Something about seeing a F18 take off just paralyzes us in our tracks. We stand there amazed. Mike can't understand it, but we feel like we're on another planet. It's a different life in the military. Very structured. His base is nothing like I pictured it. I pictured tents and tanks. This was a little community. But we were looked upon as "nasty civilians". That is how the Marine Corps thinks of us. Nasty, lazy and undisciplined. Michael took us to his room. I'm not sure what I am expecting. I guess something like a dorm room. I am correct in one aspect. The size. Other than that, it is disgusting in a mother's opinion. The bed was old and the mattress sunk in the middle and was dirty. The floor which was carpeted with some kind of outdoor carpet was filthy. The blinds were broken on one window and so my son covered it up with a sheet. I was in a word, in shock. My son thought it was home sweet home. Michael assured me that his room was clean. He pointed to the cleaning supplies he had. I have room inspection you know, he informed me. Or as they call it in the Marine Corp – Field Day.

John shot me a look that said, "Leave him alone", this is fine, and they all live this way. Cut me some slack, what I really feel like doing is going to your Sgt and requesting another, cleaner more humanly habitable room. I smile and nod my head instead. But later on that day, we head to Target to buy a foam mattress pad and a new bedspread. God knows what is lurking in the mattress!

Michael introduces us to his friend, Stanton. I was to learn only two years later that his first name was Josh. For the next two years, he was called Stanton. Nice first name I thought. Seeing Michael and Stanton together was a comfort to me. I realize that this was Mike's best friend in the Military. So this was the person he spent with these last few months this summer, fishing, batting cages, fixing his car and working with. Stanton was a firefighter as well and would be going to Iraq the same timeframe as Mike.

We did all the usual touristy things. We went to the famous San Diego Zoo where Stanton proceeded to amuse us and act like a Gorilla. They laughed and acted like 19 year olds. Sometimes like 6 year olds! So this is who is going to protect our country John said with humor. Stanton accompanied us 24/7 that entire week. His family was not going to be visiting him anytime soon and so we were his surrogate family for the time being anyway.

Courage & Faith

At the end of the week, we ask Michael if he needed anything for Iraq. He had a list of things that are "suggested" by the military that they don't supply. We learn that he is going to a base in the middle of Iraq. The list read the usual, toiletries etc, and a Ka-bar. Ka-bar? "What is that" I wondered. Sounds like a protein bar maybe to keep up their energy level?" It's a knife" John informed me. So we went shopping at the store on base for these items. It seems surreal to me. While other parents with college age kids this August are in stores standing in front of a rack of backpacks and refrigerators, I am standing there with my husband and my 19 year old son looking a rack of Knives! What's wrong with this picture? What's wrong is, I feel that everyone should have a stake in the freedom of this country and that we indeed should have a draft. All our children should be made to serve their country for at least two years. I don't mean this to sound bitter, but it should be up to everyone to have a stake in this country if we all want a military to protect us. I don't say this out loud at the moment, what I do say to my son is "Get the biggest one". I don't care what the cost, get the biggest, sharpest knife". Other mothers are imagining their sons chugging back a few beers that they will stick in their new refrigerator, I imagine my son stabbing an insurgent who is trying to kill him. I am comforted he has his knife.

Eileen Gelsomini

Our very last day before we were to leave, we ate our last meal. John and Stanton talked about the Red Sox. Mike sat in silence most of the time. I knew why and John did as well only we tried our best to hide our emotions. We dropped Stanton off at his room that night. Mike came back to the Hotel with us. He did not want to come in. We said our "good-bye's in the parking lot. I will never forget it. How can I possibly explain to someone what it feels like to say good-bye to your only son and hug him for what may be the last time. I guess only a parent whose son is going to war can know that, or a parent with a sick child can know that. I told my son earlier in the day to shoot anything that moves. I don't care if it is a woman holding a baby. In this war, they've been known to conceal weapons on women and children. Just shoot I tell him. Now I know that people who are reading this will gasp, especially mothers, but if they were in the same position I was in, they would think the same thing. "Mom", my son replied, "I can't, ..Rules of engagement". Rules of engagement in the military state that you can't fire, unless fired upon. This is only one of the politically correct "rules" we have I soon learn, that I don't agree with. Someone in Washington, who does not have a loved one in the Military probably made this rule I guess. But I would soon rather see my son alive and court-martialed, than dead. Plain and simple. So I say it and mean it. We hug Michael tightly and watch as Michael drove away in his truck. Was that the last time I will ever see my only son? When his truck is no longer in sight, I turn to John, my knees buckle underneath me and we both cry holding onto each other.

CHAPTER 7
First Deployment

August 2004 – Deployment to Iraq

The day is fast approaching for Michael to leave this country. He'll be traveling for about 3 days to get to Iraq. He will go to Germany first, then onto Kuwait, then convoy to his base in Iraq. Convoy.. I hate that word. In the news, that is the last word in a sentence that began. "3 Marines were killed in al Anbar province in a convoy".

Michael informs us that he has no idea when he will be able to call us. Maybe he'll get the chance in Germany.

D-Day.

I take the day off from work. I do not want to miss his phone call. I don't know when he will be calling. He

Courage & Faith

had to pack up his belongings and put them in storage back in San Diego and so he does not have his cell phone. We gave him plenty of phone cards. We do not hear from Mike during the day. He had told us he will probably call at night after dinner. I know this, but I took the day off anyway. I could not bring myself to go to work and deal with clients all day making small talk. John and I went to bed that night. I prayed Mike would call us. The phone rang around 10pm.

For some reason is sounded louder than usual. I picked up the phone, and John ran into the kitchen. The phone call was brief as most of the Marines needed to use the phone and the lines were long. He called from Germany. He was in the airport and they had a few hours to kill before taking off again. He sounded Ok, tired, but Ok. The phone call was brief. We repeated over and over, for him to stay safe, and told him how much we loved him and how proud we were of him. He said I love you too and that he had to go. We hung up. John walked back into the bedroom. We were both crying now. Is that the last time I would hear my son's voice? Again, another moment I felt like this was a bad dream. We slept fitfully the rest of that night. We had no idea when we would hear from Michael again. We did hear that they have e- mail, but depending on what type of base they were on, we weren't sure how accessible a computer would be. So we wait.

I went to work the next day. No one said anything. My husband went to work the next day as well. He

Eileen Gelsomini

found a little more compassion during his day. Everyone asked if he heard from his son. Of course, John is a little more vocal in this department. He seeks comfort from people and therefore mentions it to everyone. He does this mainly because he is so proud of Mike. I don't mention this because I put myself into my "denial mode". This is how I cope. That night, John put up the Service Star flag in our picture window and on our front door. We received one of the service star flags from the Veterans Dept. in town. It made me feel like someone cared. I will soon come to find that it is the people we least expect that ask about my son in Iraq. I am not sure of the reason. Maybe it has to do with my co-workers being uncomfortable bringing up the subject. Maybe it is because most of them are single and don't know the love a parent has for a child, but I suspect it is because it is the farthest thing from their minds and they don't care that much for the news or world events. What I do find out is that most of my co-workers care more about the TV show American Idol that the war. During these 7 months, I can probably count on one hand the number of times someone has asked about Michael. Maybe part of that is my fault, because I never bring it up and I come into work acting like all is well.

Most of my good clients ask about Mike more so than my co-workers, and a few have even teared up right along with me. I do not ever get political as I find out that most of my clients share opposing views from my own. Sometimes I will get a client that I've never had and when they find out about Michael over in Iraq, they will say something like "I'll say a prayer for him", or ask what his name is and say a prayer. This never fails to bring tears to my eyes. Sometimes people will voice their political views to me and say things like "we shouldn't be over there or something negative about our President. Do people think that by saying things like this, it comforts me? They must think so and think I feel the same way, but in truth it only makes me feel worse. He is over there, and we are at war.

I find the behavior of people amazing sometimes.

Here is a poem that my daughter wrote one day. It was a poem written for her brother before his first deployment. I thought it was beautiful and had it published in a Book of Poems for my daughter. She wrote it for herself actually while in her car, waiting for one of her classes. I sent it to Mike.

Eileen Gelsomini

A SISTER SAYS GOODBYE.

Your sea bag all packed up
Filled with anticipation and fear of war
It's only moments before you must leave and begin your journey
But I'm not ready
I can't give you away to the place of terror.
The place where the devil roams and his children feed on our soldiers
But it's also the place of hope
For the innocent to live in peace with no worries
You and your fellow troops are their heroes.
Rebuilding their nation to fill with their dreams
If only our country knew your good deeds
We are a country too focused on appearances
Too afraid to look within
The soldiers are the only ones with pride
But I have pride in you
In all the American troops
You may be far from home, but not far from my heart
I believe in what we are fighting for, though no one else does
Remember how proud I am of you
How much I pray for you
How much I love you
So God Bless you and all the troops.

Courage & Faith

We don't hear from Michael for some time. It is strange how you get accustomed to not hearing from one of your children. I finally receive an email at the end of September from the Cpl in charge of my son's unit.

Dear Family and Friends

My name is Cplt Guthrie. I am responsible for your loved ones during their tour in Iraq. (I have to mention that Cplt Guthrie I was soon to find out is only 23 years old!)

My purpose in writing to you is to let you know that I am going to be sending each of you an update on how we are doing, what is going on and other newsworthy information. My intention is to keep you informed of our situation out here to make things easier at home for you the parents and spouses. I will try to send e mail weekly. (That never happened, but it was a nice thought!) *One month has passed and your marines have proven themselves to be exceptional crash crewmen. When we first arrived here in August this camp was a mess. Crash fire and Rescue had to assume responsibilities on equipment that was in complete disarray. The firefighters we relieved had no fire response standards in place and no fire plan in place. Even their living conditions were unsat. In a few short days your marines turned all that around CFR (Crash, Fire, Rescue) can respond to anywhere on the camp in less then five minutes. We are also able to get five people out of an aircraft in an emergency situation in under one minute, that is an amazing feat.*

Eileen Gelsomini

Everyone sends their love and can't wait to get home. Lcptl Johnson sends his love to his wife, Tiffany, PFC Gelsomini will be promoted next month to the rank of Lance Corporal. LCplt Jackson and Cplt Guthrie both had birthdays. Both received a pound cake with a candle on it. Thank you for all of your continued love and prayers and support.

Cpl Guthrie.

I wrote back.

Thank you so much for this update. As parents we are so concerned about how our son is doing ie. Is he safe, healthy, lonely, etc? Mike Gelsomini's birthday is November 7th and so we hope you'll spread the word, so maybe someone can wish him a happy birthday. He will be 20 years old. We pray you all stay safe and come home in March as planned. Thank you all so much for serving over in Iraq. Semper fi, John and Eileen Gelsomini

Dear John and Eileen

Pfc Gelsomini is doing great. He is a very smart person and is a pleasure to have around. I know there is probably nothing I can say to completely assure you that he is safe, but he is indeed very safe. And I can guarantee that he is not lonely, he lives in a room with three other guys if anything he would like more alone time. I will relay that you love and miss him.

Cpl. Guthrie

Courage & Faith

I kept reading that one line over and over again. "I can assure you that he is indeed very safe. Now I know that he cannot possibly assure me anything, especially that Mike is safe. But I believe him. It makes me feel better.

Hey mom and dad,

Today is a crummy day. Big ass sand storm and we can't do anything. It gets over everything. This month is some Iraq religious holiday and we lost all of our workers on base so now we can't use porta potties so we have ditches and people have to go around and collect the drums and burn the crap everyday and collect the trash. We can't shower until further notice. We are tightening up security because terrorist believe that if they die killing Americans that they go to heaven for free so we have to watch for that because they found out some stuff in town. But don't worry, we are managing, don't worry. Love u Mike.

Hello Everyone:

It is time for another update to you the families of my troops. Since I wrote last a lot of changes have taken place at Mudyasis. We are losing the Iraqi nationals that were on the base to take the trash and burn it, to clean the porta potties, and bring us water. So right now we are not going to be able to shower every day and our laundry might not get washed for a while. As for our rest rooms, we will be digging a trench and you can imagine from there, so things out here are going to get a little rough for a while. PFC Gelsomini was promoted to the rank of Lance Corpora since I wrote last. The guys have been driving the fire trucks around well racing the fire trucks around. Proving we will have fun in the worst of times. Lcpt. Gelsomini and Lcpt Johnson spend their days hunting Camel Spiders and Scorpions they have found. Personally I think they are brave to go out looking for them! Cpl Guthrie.

Hey mom and dad,

*Its raining pretty good right now and the lightening in the desert is so cool. Things are good. I am now on one of our two react teams which are made up of the best guys on camp. We just started drills mainly cause they think we are going to get attacked soon. I tried to volunteer to carry the M240 **golf** a huge machine gun but our corporal got it. We did bad ass on our drill today without any warning and we moved with intensity and speed to man our trucks and get to the edges of base that's being attacked and pick up wounded. I miss everyone so much I just can't wait to come home and I am just trying to do my best out here and kick ass for my country. Love mike.*

Ps how are the sox doing? I watched the cardinal's game, I am the only sox fan out here.

Hey mom and dad,

Just got off tower duty. No sleep. It's freezing up there in the tiny ass tower. It's high up and its like 5x5. We got good night vision goggles though so it's ok to spy on towns around us but I am so tired, I got like 4 hours till my next duty so I'll talk to you later. Love mike

CHAPTER 8
Mid Deployment

October is normally the best time of the year for me. I should start to prepare for Thanksgiving and Christmas but I can't even think about those things now. My mind is not on anything. Not on work, my family or the Holidays. Everyone around me though is oblivious to what is going on inside of me. If someone does ask about Mike, I tell them it's hard and change the subject.

It's a beautiful fall day outside. John decided to take me for a ride to get my mind off of things and his as well. While we are driving all I feel like doing is staring out the window. My eyes start to fill up and John notices. "Eileen", If I tell you something do you promise to not say anything", John said to me. What is it? I ask. Dave is going to ask Valerie to marry him" my husband tells me. When? How do you know? How

Courage & Faith

long have you known? All at once I blurt out these questions. That's one thing about John, he can keep a secret. I've known since about August he informs me. "August"? You knew a few months ago and you didn't tell me.?" "Well Dave told me not to say anything to anyone. I just thought I would tell you because you looked so depressed and I wanted to cheer you up". My eyes start to fill up again. This time out of happiness. My daughter is going to get engaged! I can't believe it. We start to speculate on when Dave will ask her. Well John's plan worked. It got my mind off of Michael and onto planning a wedding. Now all I had to do was wait. John wondered if he opened up a can of worms. Knowing me, I would not only worry about Michael, I would start to worry about the wedding. But he took a chance. I'm excited! And I admit it. I thought of nothing else that entire ride.

Hey, Sup (e mail slang for "what's up")

Last night of duty and its going by so slow. The guy I am on duty with is cool. We've talked about so much to pass the time. It's that way with so many marines whenever you are on duty it always happens you just shoot the breeze and end up telling your life story and plans. I never knew he was a thug back home and had to carry a gun everywhere. I've met so many types of people, but he's my bud though. I can't wait to get home, its gonna be like boot camp all over again. They are already asking who wants to extend out here for another 6 months. Screw that, no one wanted to ha, ha. Love mike

November

Hey what's Up, How is shit at home? I can't wait to get out of this fucker. It is so hard to respond back to your e mails because both our Sgt's are on the computers nonstop. So it's so hard to get on with enough time to read them. I'm just sitting hotspot right now. I'll be out here until six tonight and it's like 8am. We have a new schedule. One crew sits hotspot all day and the other is base crew all day and it rotates from there. It's alright some days. Other days it's tiring as fuck sitting hotspot all day. Base crew does fire inspections half the days. You get to see how nasty people live. Almost the halfway point. I need to get outta here. I can't take it. Its all bullshit and drama here. It's like fucking high school where everyone is a fucking child. No one treats each other like a man or a human. Can't wait to get home. Wanna be a fucking civilian again with a nasty beard and my dickies. Gotta find a normal job for a little bit till I get hired. I have no idea. Josh said if I can't find anything I can do his uncles construction company till I get onto a department. I just want a normal life for a little before I get into a uniform again. You don't understand the toll it takes mentally. It turns you into a hateful person. It desensitizes you to the point where you don't care about shit. People dying means nothing to you and seeing death out here ain't shit either. I've off loaded so many dead marines off birds and it's fucked up. The only feeling Marines have is hate. It's hard to explain but it's fucked up who the Marines make you. Need a normal day job for a little to get some sanity. 24/7 duty sucks. We got beer for the USMC birthday. Couldn't drink it. Its awesome waiting 30 minutes in line just to get rejected in front of everyone. I don't want anything for Christmas. Well I'll go on with my shitty life.

Love mike

Here is another letter he wrote the same day

I feel so shitty being here. I feel like I'm here and everyone else's life back home is going on without me. I miss out on everything. Everything. I hear about everything going on back home and I get so pissed. I come home and I'm an outsider. Its weird like I've only been home a couple of times and I will have a brother in Law and I've been around him like three times. It just sucks. Like all these family things with Val and Dave and Steph and Nick and I'm in California or Iraq. The only time its normal is when I'm home and I'm with Lori and we do the whole family thing.

Eileen Gelsomini

My son must have been in such a bad place when he wrote this letter. Seen so many things that we at home would find unimaginable. I look around at my clean house, beautiful backyard, and nice life. And then I listen to people complain about the most idiotic things in life. I want to take this letter with me and tell them to read it. I feel so bad for my son and I can't do anything about it. I thank God he has his girlfriend Lori to vent to as well.

Hey, what's up?

How's the U.S? Just sitting in my tower freezing watching for assholes that wanna come and kill my Marines. Being out here on guard duty, you just chill and shoot the crap with the other guy. You gotta learn to trust him with your life in the tower. It's still hard to get used to carrying a loaded rifle a lot of places. We are losing a couple of crash crew guys and we are scared at what kind of guys that will replace them. My buddy is staying though. His wife is having a baby and he just found out it's a girl. His last name is Johnson so we give him shit about his kid's names like they should be Hairy Johnson and stuff like that! It's funny. I can't wait to come home and do anything I want. Its gonna be awesome. Love mike

Courage & Faith

I came home from work one day to find a voicemail from Mike. I felt so bad that I missed his call. He sounded upset that we weren't home and said that they are shutting down phone lines and all communication for a while. Also that he can't tell us what is going on but that he loves us. I saved his message on my answering machine so I could always hear his voice. I didn't want to delete it because if he did not make it home, I would at least have his voice that I could play over and over again. I know this sounds morbid, but it's what I did. I immediately called John and told him what Mike said and we figured he was going out on a mission. John and I would worry until we heard from him again. When? I didn't know. When I say worry, I'm not talking about the kind of worry you have when you hand your son the car keys for the first time. Take that worry and times it by a thousand.

We received a call from Mike's girlfriend, Lori. She said that Mike was allowed a phone call and tried to call us. Mike asked his girlfriend to tell us that he loves us very much.

So now we wait. Whatever is happening over there will probably be in the news sooner or later. I can't believe that we missed Mike's phone call. Was that going to be the last phone call he will ever make to us? Would that have been the last time we would have heard his voice? I don't sleep at all tonight. We received this e mail a few weeks later.

Eileen Gelsomini

Hey mom and dad,

Yeah, I have no clue when you'll get this. They took away our email and phones for everyone in Iraq. Now we can't go anywhere without having our flack jacket and Kevlar helmet and gas mask. Some shit is about to go down and I can't say, so that's why our contacts are gone, so it doesn't get leaked. But the time you get this you'll probably have seen it on the news or maybe I'll have called. This makes everything suck and who knows what's going to happen to us out here. How are things at home? Is everyone doing good? I don't know how this is going to make things, I just hope you don't freak out because you haven't heard from me in a long time. Love mike

Too late – It has been a while before we received that e mail. And yes, Mike, I did "freak out". It's been tough for all of us at home, waiting for some word from you that you are all right. They have launched a huge offensive in Iraq. All communications have been shut down, again. John and I can't sleep. I can eat, however and by the time this deployment is over, I'll have gained about 8 pounds. Food is my only comfort during the times that John can't be there for me because he is also stressing big time. Dinnertime we try to act normal. When the subject of Mike comes up, it's the usual, "how is he, have you heard from him". We appreciate that very much. But when we tell them, that this time, things are going down over there, and Mike may be in the thick of it, and we have no way of knowing, they really don't know what to say, understandably. This war affects them differently and doesn't really hit that close to home. They mean well when they try to reassure us. I love my family for that. But in all honesty, they can't realize the fear we have every day until we hear from him again. The fear just doesn't go away, it's there when you wake up and when you go to sleep and sometimes during the night. This particular time, though, I was extremely worried. My father informs us that we are lucky. Lucky because during WWII parents never heard from their children, there was no such thing as e- mail. I guess in that aspect we are luckier. But it's still one of those things that really doesn't matter much to me now.

We received this letter in the mail from Mike after we knew he was Ok from emails. Mail takes approximately 4-8 weeks to get here, depending on situations. I cried after I read his letter to us. I read it over the phone to John at work. I can't even imagine what is going through my son's mind as he is writing this. I want him home.

Hey great family

Yeah I just tried to call, anyway I called to let you know shit is going down, the biggest movement since Hue City 40 years ago. Communication in Iraq is yanked for a long time. So I was upset as hell when I got no answer.

I called Lori and yea she'll let you know because this letter will take a long ass time to get to you. I don't know what's gonna happen to us here so just in case, I don't know I might just be talking shit but a lot of shit can happen in the time I can't talk to you all. In case it does you are the best family in the world, I love each and everyone of you, always remember that and I'm glad I'm doing what I can to keep you guys safe. You have all taught me so much in life and its stuff I use or remember everyday in life. You have all shaped my life in some way. I love you for that. So if I don't make it home from this fucked up piece of shit country, then always remember you are all big influences on my life. Love mike.

He wrote this letter, thinking there may be a chance he wouldn't make it. I will always cherish this letter, along with every single e mail.

Everyone has been so great in sending Michael packages. John's aunts and cousins have all sent packages. My family has sent packages and letters. They will never know how much this means to me. Never. My good friend, Eileen, drove to Hudson, Ma and took pictures of our hometown and sent them to him. The road home was what she wrote. I can't believe she drove all the way up here and took those pictures. The kindness of some people, never fail to amaze me. And this touches me very much.

Courage & Faith

I ask God for the strength to get through these last four months. I ask him to bless us all and please, please bring Michael back home to us safely. Before Michael left for Iraq, a co-worker gave me a stone with an angel on it. It's a prayer stone, she told me. Her son was in the Navy and just got out year ago. Whenever you are stressed or worried about your son, take it out and hold it and pray. I pray with it everyday and keep it in my purse always. Sometimes I hold it as I drive to work and pray. I will pray on this angel stone the entire 4 years.

CHAPTER 9
Homestretch

Well it's December. Another three months and my son will be home. I keep focusing on that. John's birthday is December 8th and John wonders if he may receive a call from Michael. I know John is not getting his hopes up. Still is would be nice to hear from Mike. What am I talking about; it would be terrific to hear his voice. December 8th comes and goes and I know John is disappointed.

December 9th,

Hey Dad, I'm so sorry about yesterday, I was trying to time it to call you on your birthday during the day and I got it all mixed up because the corporals have been putting a lot more responsibility to get things done so I was all stressed out and shit cause they are doing it for a good reason. So I wanted to do it all right and I forgot to call when I was supposed to wish you a happy birthday. I'm sorry dad. I love you. Oh yeah, I freaked out, I got your package yesterday, thank you two so friggin much. That shit is awesome, thank you. Love mike

I guess we must have sent some more cigars to him. When he smokes them it reminds him of fishing with John. We haven't heard from him in about a week and so John and I are worried. We are wondering what he is doing and where he is. It's a different kind of worry that parents have from lets say, worrying about if your child is Ok at college or living away from home somewhere in another state. That child may be at the movies or hanging out with friends or shopping. Our worry is that Mike is off on maneuvers somewhere doing God knows what. It's a feeling that only my husband understands. It's getting old thinking this way and it's taking its toll. John and I are just going through the steps everyday of waking up, going to our jobs and coming home to watch the news. Any real happiness in our lives at this point is offset by this feeling of dread we both have on a daily basis. We can't explain this to anyone and sometimes we don't even share it with each other. I feel bad thinking this way.

I know he feels the same way. I know that when he is laughing at something with someone, it's fake. I know this because this is the way I feel as well. I guess its survival.

Eileen Gelsomini

Hi Mike,

Your father and I are somewhat worried here. We haven't heard from you in almost a week. Can you just shoot us a quick e-mail to let us know that you are Ok, please? We are hoping that either you are very busy or have guard duty or maybe the e-mail is down or something but as soon as you can, just a quick, "I'm Ok". We love you very much, Mike, please stay safe. Love mom

It is a few weeks before Christmas. One afternoon we receive a phone call from a very excited Valerie. Val and Dave have gone ice skating in Boston and Dave had proposed. That bit of news lifted my spirits considerably. Val was surprised and Dave had a friend nearby who had taken a picture of Dave proposing to Val. We have that picture in our living room. I love it because it is so candid and you can see real happiness there. So I will have something happy to focus on. We start to plan the wedding!

I email Mike to give him the news. Hopefully he gets it. I think back to his comment on feeling like life is going on without him at home.

Hey Mom and Dad,

Yeah, you are right, I am on guard duty but I was also gone doing some other shit. Um yeah. Guard duty is so friggin cold at night and in the morning. It was 30 today and with the wind-chill about 20. I'm 30 feet up. Tell

Val congratulations with the proposal, that's awesome. How did he do it? You said something about Boston. Yea trying to work the wedding around me might be hard as hell. I didn't know what you had in mind here, but yeah, I'll try my ass off to call, but that's good news about Val.

Hi Mike,

I'm glad you emailed, we were very worried. I know if I ask you where you were for a couple of days you won't tell us right? But I just called your father to ease his mind and let him know that you did e mail us. Because he cried last night. His job is so stressing we haven't heard from you and I had to give him a full body massage. He is ok now that I have called him. Sometimes he cries and I comfort him and am strong and sometimes I cry and breakdown and he is strong for me. But all I know is this sucks. So we will tell Val to try and plan her wedding maybe in the fall a few months after you get back in March. I think you'll be here right? Because you mentioned that you won't be going again for at least a year when you get back. He took her ice skating and then proposed. She is all excited and they are coming to dinner tomorrow night at our house. Don't worry about calling, we know you are busy, but we were both so worried that we didn't hear from you in a while and either has Lori. Now your father and I can relax a little today because I thought I'd have a breakdown this morning. I kept turning on the e mail. Anyway mike, please. Stay safe, we love you very much, miss you so much love mom

Eileen Gelsomini

12/19

Hey Mom and Dad, what's up, yea I've been really busy lately with guard and shit. I wrote a couple of letters. I got a package from Uncle Paul that had some bad ass cigars. I smoked that nice Cohiba last night and it made me remember when we went fishing that was bad ass. I wish I could be with you fishing right now and ha ha mom, we gotta go to the gun range, ha ha. Yeah dad, I got that package with the straps and shit, fucking awesome, thank you guys. I love you guys so much and I miss you all so much, tell everyone I said hi, igtg, love mike

Yeah should be home by the 27th of Feb, but we are convoying back, Yes hope I can get some more action than I've been getting. Not enough, but we are getting some good shit, but I got some bad ass stories for home about that. I'm hearing mixed things about re-deploying, now it may be September 2006.

I'm beginning to wonder if my son will be there for his sisters' wedding. This will break my heart if he can't be home for a few days for that. You never know in the Marine Corp. You may have some Sgt who may or may not care about Michael attending his sisters' wedding. Michael doesn't seem to paint a promising picture. But I am not one to take no for an answer. I have plans of my own. Plans that I don't even tell John about.

We are starting to think about Mike's homecoming. It's not even Christmas yet. I guess we are thinking ahead to make the time go by faster. I am going to do my best to make this a good Christmas. I decorate the inside of the house halfheartedly. If I could go to sleep now and wake up the day after Christmas that would be just fine with me.

12/24

Hey what's up? Yeah it really doesn't feel remotely like Christmas. I forgot it was Christmas eve today. I might as well not think about it. Probably got flights all day and shit. All I want for my Christmas present is my packages I'm waiting on from people who sent them to me and to get to the gym today. Well I hope you guys have a great Christmas. Love mike,

I did mail Mike his Christmas package about a month ago. In it I put a tiny Christmas tree. I wrapped his gifts so he would have something to open. Space is so limited there and so he had asked me and anyone else to just send small articles. I sent him a watch, and then I wrapped some tuna packages, some candy and other small items. How pathetic.

December 24th,

I know that's its Christmas where you are right now. We just came from Aunt Sandra's, we had a good time. Thanks for calling us today, it made our day. I think that its 6:30am xmas morning where you are. I hope you have a nice day with all of your friends. We thanked Uncle Steve and Sandra, Paul and Paula for you. Mike we miss you and love you very much. Love you and miss you, simper fi, love dad

December 25th,

Well at least we heard from Mike Christmas Eve. It is Christmas Day. Stephanie is home with us and her boyfriend Nick will be coming by later on. Val and Dave are spending Christmas Day with Dave's family. I feel bad, but can't wait for this day to be over. I know I shouldn't wish my life away like that. But it's just one day.

12/26
Hi Mike

How was your xmas? Did you get the steak and lobster with a beer? Hope your day went well. We all missed you very much. It was nice to talk to you on Saturday. I will get that package to you this week. Hang in there Mike; we are counting down the days to see you. Your mother and I watched the news yesterday and they had soldiers on TV. Wishing their families a merry xmas. I know you said you would not be in that, but we watched anyway. We cried so much because we wanted you with us. We are going to look at wedding halls today with Dave and Val.

Love you and miss you,
Simper fi
Love dad, I'm proud of you mike

12/26
Hey Dad,

Just chilling on phone watch. Had to rush through the gym today because we had a late call from the infantry needing to burn shit so we had to supervise at the burn pit. We had fuels hook it up with 216 gal. of fuel. We have an even bigger burn that we are anticipating in a few days. Yeah Christmas sucked. We had gay ass flights and shit but at night we got beer but to get it we had to come in and sit on Santa's lap while his elf took pics, ha ha. So embarrassing with suits and shit, ha ha. We got two buds (Budweiser's) and a shot of rum. Good shit. It's been a long time, so we all got a little buzzed and we made a nice little fire and all of us guys, like 30 of us screwed around all night. Love mike

Hey what's up? Yea, I forgot to mention we had a nice dinner it was some chicken and good ass steak with shrimp and corn and fucking good ass cheesecake.

1/1/05

Hey Mom and Dad, what's up, just got done with pt. Just ran a small hike 2.5 miles. Some good cardio. How have you guys been doing? Staying healthy, eating good? Yeah it's hard out here cause we can't really pick our own food. I think tonight we might get lobster or some shit for new years. Yeah I tried to send some pics from x-mas but I don't know computers and I couldn't send them. I think I'll try again. I love you guys miss you all so much and think about you all day. Oh year we are convoying back but I can't really give the date over unsecured lines but I think we should be home or on the way home on a plane around the 27 of March. Love mike.

1/3/05

Hey how's it going? Bored on phone watch. Someone put a gay ass movie on and I'm stuck watching it and the people in here are pissing me off playing a game. Someone's chewing gum so loud and popping it and I wanna kill him. I got those pictures today and it made me so homesick. I like the ones with everyone around the x-mas tree. A couple of flights today. The goddamn ch-53's like almost landed on top of us and we got sand blasted from the rotors. That shit hurts like bad. The rotors have a span of 76 feet and they kick up and throw a lot of shit. We just had a big monopoly game and I got fucked pretty quickly. Fuckers plotted against me cause I was loaded with money and talking so much shit. We had gross ass hamburgers for chow; they were all dry and shit so that sucked. I gotta change your eating habits if you are all polishing off gallons of ice cream in one night. You gotta eat good, you're both getting older. I'll set you all straight. I'm so tired and worn out, I'm getting no sleep tonight or this weekend and we gotta busy day tomorrow. I'm still doing good showing my Cpl and Sgt I can handle responsibility and stay squared away. I'm hoping I can get meritorious cplt when I get back. I thought I was going get it out here, I was really thinking I was but this base is always forgotten so our gunnies back at TQ didn't give crash crew out here an opening for it. Love mike

Letter in Mail
Hey mom and Dad, How's shit at home. I love you guys. I miss home so much right now. I got word that we should be leaving Feb 27. Bad news for you guys is I'm convoying back. I should be riding in a hummer with Cpt Langley so that's good. I got some really good stories for home, some stuff I can't tell you about till later. I smoked that nice ass Cohiba you sent me last night. It was awesome. Reminded me of when we went fishing that's the best. I still have those pics on my phone. I know you guys have been stressed out at work lately, you said in e mails but keep kicking ass. You two are great parents and I try my best to work hard at everything like you guys do here. If they had a corporal's board out here my corporal said they would have put me on it. Cause I work hard and I am locked on and squared away. Which pisses me off because non one cared about this camp out here enough to have a corporal's board. But I'll keep it up, maybe back in the states. That is wicked awesome about Val and Dave, that's some good news. How's steph going in school? Tell Val and steph I love them, I think about everyone all the time. I'm gonna go get some sleep now; I got my last guard shift tonight. Love
Lcpt Michael Gelsomini, USMC.
Ps- If possible are you coming out when I get back?

Are we coming out when he gets back?? What is he kidding? Is the Pope Catholic?!!

Of course John and I are planning to fly out there to San Diego. It is tricky with the timing however, so we need to wait for further instruction and dates from Mike.

1/12/05

Um year we might convoy the 11th if we can get shit sent out fast enough. Yeah, I'll be pissed if we get no leave. It's not us, it's the gay ass station is pushing to get us there with no leave, they don't give a shit about us, so hopefully we get someone to fight for us. I won a contest today. Me and my buddy went to see who could put 50 sticks of gum in their mouths the fastest. I won. It was so fucked up. Well igto love you

I have a map of Iraq on my refrigerator and I check it whenever I hear of a death in a certain part of Iraq. I have an idea of where Mike is. The news is on almost 24/7 at our house. We watch it for about 2 hours in the morning, I put it on when I get home in the afternoon, and it is on right after dinner until bedtime. Every day soldiers and Marines are dying. Helicopters are crashing. But we need to know what is going on. One particular morning after John left for work there is a breaking story on the news. A Helicopter is shot down in the desert West of Baghdad. Mike is west of Baghdad. The crew on board were all

Marines from the 3rd Marine Air Wing. Mike is a Marine from the Third Marine Air Wing.

I feel dizzy and panic. I immediately call John who had heard the same thing on the news. I can't sit still and start to pace around the living room. My God, please, please, don't let it be Michael, I say out loud. Stephanie came out of her bedroom and I tell her what I heard. I checked the e- mail earlier that morning and I heard nothing from Mike. I keep watching the news, waiting and waiting for some kind of information that may help me find out anything. I watch the news for about an hour. It is almost time for me to leave for work. I consider not going. I can't take it anymore. I want to quit. How am I supposed to go to work knowing that there is a good possibility that my son is dead? How? I have started to cry and rock myself on the kitchen chair. I pray, like I have never prayed before. I keep watching the news for updates. John told me to call with any other news. About an hour passes and I decide to go downstairs for one last time to check the e-mail. John told me to email Mike and hope that we hear from him soon. As soon as I turn on the computer, I see that someone had e mailed me. When I open it up it is from Mike, real time. He just e mailed me! To say I was relieved would be an understatement. I say his name out loud, put my head on the computer table and cry. I quickly answer his e mail and he does inform me that he is indeed ok and wasn't obviously on board, but a Sgt from his base was supposed to be, and at the last minute they decided that they didn't have room for him. He tells me not to worry. I sign off, and call John. Just another morning in the life of a Marine Mom.

When I went to work that morning, I was greeted by the usual "Hi Eileen, how are you?

I'm fine and you?" I reply. I couldn't possible even begin to explain

1/27/05

Hi Mike, I'm so sorry about your fellow Marines. We were so worried that something bad might have happened to you. It was a 3rd Marine wing Support. That's all we needed to hear. I told your mother to e mail you right away and you got right back to her. Thanks for the e mail. Well I have to shovel snow now and make dinner. Your mother is working later. Can't wait to see you, semper fi, love dad

1/27/05

Hey yeah I'm fine. It's cool. The crash was close to us though. I wish we could have responded and helped but we didn't know about it.

1/31/05

Yeah, that helo that crashed. it almost had one of our sergeants on it. He was about to step on and they told him there was no room. It crashed near one of our bases. It has 30 fully loaded Marines. I guess it was bad cause there was

like no way you could tell what kind of helo it was. And the crash crew had 31 body bags and 10 bags of just parts, I guess pretty shitty. Love mike

1/31/05

Hey dad, yea I guess elections went well. We had some on our base so yeah, there were a bunch left over ballots. So we got some. Its bad ass, we got the ballots of the first election of a new power in Iraq. Its cool, they are crazy looking. Love mike

2/3/05

Yea, I almost died yesterday, twice. We do all the burning on base cause we are firefighters so if someone needs important documents destroyed we burn extra wood and pallets and just anything u wanna get rid of so we are leaving this base, so we are burning like everything and so we got this huge pile and we always use fuel to ignite it and one of the fuel trucks needed to empty its tank cause we can't bring it back so he pulls up next to our pit and starts draining 800 gallons of fuel, well the fucking other guys on the base burned some shit the day before and without telling us so they had some hot embers in there still, so part of the fuel ignited and we freaked the fuck out cause it was gonna ignite the stream from the truck and blow the tank up and we are standing next to it so we frantically tried to put it out cause the flame was on a big deep puddle of fuel, and every time we put dirt on it spread it or it went out then ignited again. Luckily it was JP8 it's a mix of diesel and kerosene and it burns slow at first. And then some gay ass didn't clean out his shit before he dumped it and had some .50 cal rounds in there so they go hot enough and cooked off and like the rounds fired off so we went running for cover cause we were getting hot as, how exciting, ha ha. I miss you guys so much, I'm almost there, I can't wait.

Hi mike,

Your father just left for work, I e mailed that Sgt in Miramar. I'll wait one more week to see if he has information or will email me. Then Dad wants us to make plane reservations for when you said you would be in Miramar. We'll do our best mike ok. I'm going to activate your phone soon, so it'll be ready when you come home. Can't wait. Take care mike, keep safe. I love you. We love you very much. Love mom

Hi mike,

I was just on the Dictaphone to get an update on your arrival dates. He said as of this time that you will be home on the 1st to the 3rd time frame. He called it 2nd main body. Is this you? Let us know. Love mom

Trying to find out information is nearly impossible. I realize that they have to have secure lines for this type of information. So I am being patient. We hope that the dates are within a few days of each other because we plan to take about 8 days off, a few days before and a few days after he arrives at Miramar. They can only guarantee a "timeframe" because of circumstances beyond their control. (Someone may attack the convoy, or a plane may be late or need repair before they take off from Iraq.).

Hey dad, what's up, yeah today is our last day to use the computers. I'm almost off phone watch so that's great; I just can't wait to get back in the states. When we get back and if you guys are there we might have to go buy me some civy clothes if we can't get to my truck right away. I'm so tired. I just wanna get the fuck out of this stupid country. Love mike.

That is the last e-mail we received from Mike until we saw him in San Diego.

CHAPTER 10
Homecomiing.

We have tentative dates for Mike's plane to arrive in San Diego. He must convoy out of Iraq. We worry about that with all of the roadside bombs. Then onto Kuwait, fly out to Germany or Ireland, onto Bangor Maine, and then finally home to San Diego.

The day we have been waiting for is finally here. I am so impatient that I feel like running across country instead of waiting to fly out. I have so much energy. We arrive at Logan to begin our journey to San Diego. Everything goes as planned and we check into our hotel in San Diego. The hotel is a few minutes from the base. After unpacking we head to Target to buy poster board for our Welcome Home sign for Mike. We have no idea what to expect as far as his homecoming at the Base. Will there be a handful of people? This is what I think. Because it is not a "reserve" base where all of the military are from the same area or state, and at their homecomings there are a lot of family members. Most of the family members are scattered across the country and some can't afford plane fare and hotel. This is why I think there will be about 10 people there.

We arrive at the base to find out information on what time Mike's plane is due to arrive.

The only information they can give us is what we had a few days ago. That Mike's plane will arrive either Tues. or Wed. We are hoping his plane arrives on Tuesday, so we have a few days with him as our return flight is Friday morning.

We are mentally exhausted so we grab dinner and try to sleep. The faster I go to sleep the quicker morning will be here. Kind of how a child thinks on Christmas Eve.

Tuesday morning is here. We eat a quick breakfast and hope for the best news. We clear security and head to the flight line building. When we look up at the flight board we see that Mike's plane is due to arrive at 1pm TODAY!

So we stay there. It is 9am. We are in a plane hangar and notice that they have hung a huge sign Welcoming Home Marines and Sailors. There are about 200 chairs set up and I realize that there will be a huge crowd arriving. We are told that when the plane arrives we will file out a door on the left side in front and onto the tarmac where it will be roped off. I motion to John that we are taking the first two seats nearest the door. Hours pass and it is now about 11am and we see people start trickling in. At 12pm, we are at full capacity. There are people from all different backgrounds. Young wives who looked to be about 19. Young mothers with their children and parents like us. Whites, African American and Hispanic families. Everyone is hopeful and happy. I notice that they set up some refreshments in the other room as well as some toys for the children. Definitely not what I expected. I am pleasantly surprised. They are selling T shirts and of course John and I get two.

There is some commotion going on at the front desk and soon word gets around that the plane has been delayed until 3pm. They seem to be having some mechanical difficulties with the plane. Disappointment sets in. Ok, so it's a few hours I think. Let's get some lunch and come back. Everyone files out.

After lunch we head back to the base and back to the flight building. We look at the flight monitor and now its said 7pm. So we just stay there and wait.

"You've got to be kidding" I say to my husband. John kept checking every half hour or so for updates. I see him walking towards me and I know by the look on his face that the news is not good. We find out that they are now due to arrive the following day in the afternoon. My heart sinks. You would think that they would fly them home on a decent plane.

Dinner that night is somber. John and I don't say much and our moods are "testy". We call home to Stephanie and let her know what is going on. It is such a letdown. On

Courage & Faith

Wed morning John and I arrive at the base and head straight to the hanger. The plane is still targeted for arrival in the afternoon. John and I wait there and see other people start to arrive. Well all in all, it wasn't so bad; we knew that they gave us dates a day apart to begin with.

There is another update to let us know that the plane has arrived in the states; Bangor, Maine to be exact. The crowd lets out a cheer and everyone starts clapping. Our Marines are home!!!! Safe on U.S. soil. I find myself getting emotional. Mike's plane is due to arrive in 6 hours. Everyone leaves to grab lunch or do some sightseeing. How could they eat and sightsee I think to myself. I feel like if I left the hanger, I will somehow miss the whole thing! They are the normal, reasonable people, unlike me, so John and I stay there. It is about time for people to start arriving back. We notice that they took down the arrival time for that day. Everyone is starting to look a little weary. This waiting is taking its toll. Everyone takes their seats anxiously awaiting their loved ones arrival. I see a woman in uniform entering the room going to the front looking like she is going to address the crowd.

My heart sinks again because I know this can't be good. It's not. The plane has broken down again and they are waiting for another part. They can't give us a time yet and will update us. They advise us all to go home and call instead of waiting. Most of the families stay. Everyone is impatient now and angry. " Never mind a part for the plane, get them a new plane" a father says. We all agree. After waiting for hours, we get the word that they will be spending the night in Maine and won't be home until Thursday. They don't know the time either, could be Thursday night. Our flight leaves on Friday and I am due back in work on Saturday. Most of the people there are pretty angry. I quickly call my co-worker and ask if she could cover Saturday for me. She can and I am relieved. Now the real problem is changing our flight plans. We head back to our hotel and place a call to Travelocity. They can change our plane reservation to Monday but it will cost us over a thousand dollars extra to do so. Even after we explain to them our circumstances, that is the best they can do. John and I can't believe it and we head down to the airport to the airlines our reservation is through. We head to the counter. When we explained our situation with Travelocity the gentleman behind the counter told us it would be no problem to change our reservation to depart on Monday and also will not charge us a penalty fee. We couldn't believe it and thanked him so many times. I don't know if he just took pity on us, and didn't want a scene. But I like to believe that it was because he was wearing a Vietnam Veteran Pin and was a true patriot.

Whatever the case, we were truly grateful to this man.

Thursday morning arrived. John and I eat breakfast early and in silence. Both of us realize that if this plane doesn't arrive here today, the Marine Corps will have some

Courage & Faith

explaining to do to about 200 family members! Once again we arrive at Miramar Air Base and proceed to the hanger. When we arrive the board says that our son's plane is due to arrive at 2pm. I take my seat, closest to the door. I am not moving, not even to go to the bathroom. The time is closing in on about 12pm and family members start trickling in.

At about 1pm, the place is at full capacity. Delaying this plane is not an option. We are all determined to see our sons and daughters this day. We received the news that the plane is half way across country and again the crowd lets out a cheer and we clap. People start getting up out of their seats in anticipation even though we still have a few hours. Everyone is anxious.

At about 1:30, we are given instructions that we are to file out of the hanger onto the tarmac. They will let us out when the plane is a few miles away. My idea of taking the first seats proves to be futile as mothers with baby carriages line up at the door. Damn I think to myself, how am I going to get ahead of this. Well I can't, so I am about the 10th one out the door. But I run quicker than mothers with carriages and so John and I are right up front at the ropes. All of a sudden someone yells out, there is the plane!! We look to our left and sure enough, I see a tiny little black dot. The entire crowd starts to yell and cheer and clap. My eyes start to fill up. The dot gets closer and closer until I can finally see that it is indeed the plane. We can hear it now thundering to the left of us when all of a sudden we lose sight of it in the fog, then silence. I swear it was like something out of a movie, but this huge plane breaks through the fog, decends onto the tarmac and the crowd goes wild. Signs are waving, kids are jumping, mothers are crying and wives and girlfriends are anticipating their hugs and kisses. I look at John, and he hugs me and we think God this has been some journey. This nightmare is finally over. We can't believe our Michael is on that plane. My son is on that plane.

The plane has to go all the way to the end of the runway and turn around. It seems like it is taking forever. The plane makes its way to us and finally came to a stop. If you've ever seen a science fiction movie where a spaceship lands and it takes forever for the hatch door to open to see the Martians come out, well that is what this scene is like. We wait and wait. Come on, what is taking them so long I think. Finally the door opens and the Marines start their climb down the stairs. They start to trickle out at first, then more and more start piling out. There must have been about 300 or so Marines on that plane. The crowd doesn't stop clapping until the last Marine is out which took about 45 minutes. My hands were raw. The Marines went into formation directly in front of us.

John who has better vision than me is looking for our son. They all look the same with their uniforms on.

The Marines stand in rows and John is scanning. He thinks he sees Mike and I look but really can't see him. He swears it is Michael. The Commanding General gives

Courage & Faith

a short, but very patriotic speech and then says "its all clear"; you can go hug your Marine now.

The entire lot of us, families and Marines are like tiny ants scattering around, hunting for our loves ones. I see families unite, tears, hugs. I'm frantic now, and then John calls out, "there he is, I see him, I see him, there's Michael". We make our way to Michael, shoving through the crowd. We finally make contact with our son. We hug each other and I cry. "Why are you crying" Mike said to me. I can't stop staring at him; I waited for this for so long. And just at that moment I think two things. One. How I sometimes thought that I'd never see this face again and how lucky I am, and two...all the other mothers out there who will never get to see their sons again. I reflect for a moment, out of respect and sadness. But I am here now, and I am with my son, and this is by far the best day of my life, hands down.

After all has settled down, I realize that Michael is carrying his rifle.

I've never seen a rifle in person, and it looks fake to me. I imagine my son, carrying that rifle to protect his life and those of his fellow Marines. I wonder how many times that rifle has been used and under what circumstances. Just then a Sgt whom we knew by name only introduces himself. "I just want to let you know that you have a fine son" he said to us. We shake hands and thank him for his service. We find his best friend Stanton. Stanton doesn't have his family at this homecoming and so we become his "surrogate" family for the time being.

We wait for Mike to get in line to return his rifle and retrieve his duffle bag from a huge pile. This whole process takes about 2 hours. We wait for Stanton as well. The boys have a new room assignment; they still have their vehicles to get but won't be able to get them until tomorrow.

Earlier in the week when we first arrived in San Diego, we knew Stanton did not have family out there to greet him. We knew the boys would not have any clothes or toiletries available initially and so John and I made a trip to Target to pick up some clothes for Mike and Stanton.

We first go to our hotel, so the boys can take a hot shower which must be like heaven to them. Mike explained to us that when they spent the night in Bangor, they slept in a hotel room. Also some veterans, older about 60-80 years old were there to greet them and give out some cell phones so they could call us. The Marines felt appreciated and so grateful to them.

We ate dinner and the boys were full of stories, but quite tired. Stanton wanted to find his room on the base and sleep there. Mike stayed with us. That night in our hotel, I rubbed my son's back as he lay on the bed. I hugged him. And I just looked at him.

Did I mention that this was the best day of my life?

The following morning was the start of a few days of just getting Mike and Stanton settled and getting everything they needed including their vehicles. We did some sightseeing and just ate out. We only had a few days with him and I was sad, but at least he was home now. What the future would hold, I didn't know or want to think about at this moment. Our departure was a tearful one. Mike on one hand was so glad to be back in the states, but still had another two and half years to go.

CHAPTER 11
Getting Political

Mike was getting settled into his routine as usual in San Diego. Meanwhile John was busy remodeling Val and Dave's home that they had just purchased. They had to gut the entire downstairs. Stephanie and I were busy planning Valerie's shower.

Whenever the subject of Mike being able to attend Valerie's wedding came up, it was a touchy one. Mike didn't know if he would have the time saved to attend or not or if they would even let him. This conversation went on for a few months. I would be so brokenhearted and so would Val if Mike was not there to see her get married. I think that Mike did not want to ask his Sgt if he could have the time off. Not having Mike at the wedding was not an option to me. So I did not tell anyone, not even John because if he knew what I was about to do, he would definitely not agree. I emailed the head of his unit on behalf of my 77 year old parents if they could see their grandson on this special occasion as they have not seen him in four years. And also that my father was in WWII and would like nothing more than to see his grandson in his dress blues. I received an answer via e mail that said he would see what he could do and make every effort to see that Mike would be home for his sister's wedding. I realize that most mothers would probably not go to this extent. That's just not my style.

A few weeks later, Mike got the word that he could attend, but would only be given about 4 days off for travel and the wedding. I was ecstatic and no one was the wiser as to what I did.

The first few months, I noticed that my son wasn't the same. I can't put my finger on it, but even John noticed it. Was he depressed because he knew he had over two years to go? Was he depressed because his knew he would probably be going back to Iraq? Or did he have post traumatic stress syndrome? All of the above? None of the above? All I knew was that there was something different in Mike's behavior. Sadder, maybe. I mentioned this to John several times. John who hates to admit there is a problem with anything or anyone, reluctantly agreed. "Give him some time to adjust". He went through a lot, probably things he will never talk to us about". He just needs time. But as a mother, I couldn't just 'give him time. What if we gave him too much time and he did something stupid. Ok,

I'll say it, take his life. I was that worried. I was two thousand miles away and couldn't see him or help him. Or could I? I decided not to take any chances and found the email address of one of his sergeants. The same Sgt who came up to us at the homecoming. Mike thought highly of him. I e-mailed my concerns and asked him to keep an eye out for anything distressing. Well about two weeks into that e mail, Mike called and told us that Sgt Langley came up to him and ask if he was Ok or needed help with anything. Mike thought that was odd. John was surprised as well. He had no clue that I had e-mailed Sgt. Langley. After that, Mike seemed fine. He went back to being his "old self". I don't know what else transpired between Mike and Sgt Langley, but it worked. And I felt a heck of a lot better. I didn't tell John about my e mails for a few months. A mother has to do what a mother has to do, and only a mother can understand.

We attended the Memorial Day parade and the laying of the wreath on the Hudson, Ma. Town Common. There were quite a few people there, some with little flags in their hands. It almost reminded me of when I was a child growing up on Long Island, New York and the parades we had on the 4th of July and Memorial Day. Only back then in the late 60's the entire town showed up. Not so true in 2006. There was the High School band playing, Boy Scout troops and of course the Town of Hudson fire trucks. I said to myself that

Courage & Faith

someday, Mike will be on one of those trucks. It came time for the Laying of the Wreath at the memorial for all of the men and women who have given their life for this country. My feelings were mixed between sadness, honor and being completely terrified that one day I'd be standing here honoring my son. I want to honor my son on Veterans Day, not Memorial Day. I once asked a young person at work if they knew what Memorial Day was for because we had the weekend off and everyone had plans. She gave it some thought, a few seconds too long I thought to myself, and then she said "for the dead soldiers". Ok, at least she knew the answer even thought it took her a bit to think about it.

During the summer, John and I usually take a day trip to either Ogunquit, Maine, or to the nice affluent New England town of Newburyport, Mass. Today, we chose Newburyport. John and I like to go up to walk around the harbor and check out the boats. They also have a nice little town grassy common area. People walk their dogs and have picnics. There is also a nice antique barn housing everything from furniture to dishes to antique dolls and jewelry. Truly a nice day trip. Then we have lunch as well.

This particular day was chosen by about 15 men and women to protest the war and our presence there and protest our President as well. Now we see this often in a lot of towns while driving. It's certainly not uncommon nowadays for any town in the U.S. to have protests. Right smack in the center of this town, on the corner was where these protesters chose to display their signs and at times verbalize their discontent. To this day, for reasons I can't fully explain, John and I chose to "disrupt this gathering". As we passed, John said something to one of the women holding a sign. Her sign said something about bringing the troops home. It always amazes me that it's the people who do not have a loved one over there that want them home. If the protesters ever bothered to ask an active member of the volunteer Military how they felt, the majority of them want to actually be there. John didn't yell nor did he get in her face, but simply said to her, "we can't bring the troops home yet, we need to fight the terrorist over there, so they do not come here again". With that remark her response to him was " we are the terrorist". Now I know that most people would just walk away, maybe shaking their heads, but that's not what happened here. What ensued was a yelling match by John, myself and at least a ¼ of those protesters. Each of us arguing our own points. When at last we stopped because now it was getting pretty heated. The man I was nose to nose with was twice my size and looked to me like he was going to start swinging at me. So I grabbed John and we walked away.

Not my proudest moment to say the least. But boy did I feel invigorated.

Courage & Faith

The day of Valerie's wedding was finally here.

Waking up that morning, I had my entire family with me. My daughter Valerie did not seem the least bit nervous, just happy. As we all just sat there eating breakfast, I had flashbacks to when they were just kids sitting at the table. Where did the time go?

Valerie looked so radiant in her wedding gown. We had to keep our dog, Chucky from going near her gown. It was one of those moments that was surreal, seeing her in her gown.

My son walked me down the aisle in his dress blues. I felt all eyes on us and was so proud. I watched as my beautiful daughter, Stephanie, the maid of honor, walked up towards the altar and again as my other equally beautiful daughter, Valerie in her wedding dress was escorted by John. I know all children's wedding days are special in every family, but I felt that this was special because we were all there! I will admit that it crossed my mind a few times playing out this day without my son, either because he couldn't attend or he was killed in action. Morbid I know, but this was my thought process for four years.

Christmas this year was going to be so different. We we going to San Diego to spend it with Mike. Mike asked us if we could bring a few presents for him to open. He told us he has not unwrapped a real present for some time. We were planning to give him money to help with his expenses. While they are at the fire station, Mike has to buy his own food most of the time. Because he cannot leave the station whenever he wants and most of the time the cafeteria is closed when he is off his shift. They don't make much in the corps and Mike has had to buy his own uniforms, some food for the week and even the metals or ribbons they buy for themselves. So we figured money was what he needed the most. I guess not. What Mike needed the most was a present to open.

We brought both! I found out that there is nothing like Christmas in New England. Very scenic and charming in most of the towns. Most stores and houses are decorated here in Massachusetts. We found out it is not quite the same in San Diego. We noticed very few decorations on homes and stores. Of course the weather was warmer as well. Our hotel had a huge Christmas tree however, but still all in all it seemed strange to us. We made the best of it. Christmas morning John, myself and Stephanie gave Mike his gifts to open in the hotel room. Then we went to the movies later on that day. It did not feel remotely like Christmas, but I am so glad we had the chance to spend it with Mike. We wouldn't be so fortunate in 2006.

CHAPTER 12
Second deployment

August 06 – March 07

Mike came home for about a week in the summer, right before he left for Iraq. This time John and I decided not go out to San Diego before he deploys. I can't bear it. I can't stand another good bye. This time Mike is a lot closer to Baghdad at a bigger base. This is good because the gym is bigger and they get to eat mostly real food, not so may MRE's. (Meal Ready to Eat, pre packaged military meals) Mike brought home a few once. I couldn't bring myself to eat one.

It is different with this deployment. The war is getting "old "for some people. But for us, it's so very real. It's our life. We give Mike's new address to our family. Thank God for them. They will still send him packages and letters.

That comforts me. This time I know the routine so to speak, so that's better, however, I think to myself that Mike is pushing his luck going over again. Are we going to be lucky enough again and have him come back to us safely? The thought scares the heck out of me. Not a day goes by that I do not pray every morning on my Angel Stone.

The week after Michael left John and I head out to Block Island. His cousin, Nick and Pam have a summer house there. We are invited to spend the night. John and I take them up on their offer. What perfect timing. It will get our minds off of Mike leaving. We had a good time and it did just that, gave our minds a break for two days.

Another Thanksgiving without our son home. I think they are having steak or something good. Everything this year is considered by me to be "the last time". The last time Mike will be gone for this or that. So this is the last time we spend a Thanksgiving wondering about where our son is. I just have to get through this Holiday Season one last time.

12/12/06

Yea we had no email last night. We lost 5 Marines I knew so that sucks. My living conditions aren't bad. We have a TV in our office. I'll try to call soon.

I haven't had a day off in a while. I'm taking some of those practice tests from the fire exam book. I did two 150 practice ones and now I'm grading them. Lets me know what I gotta work on. So far its ropes and knots and some other like logistics crap. Love mike

I sent Mike some firefighting practice exam books for when he comes home to take the civil service exam. I begin to send his resume out to all the towns as well as the government jobsite. I had no idea that the government had firefighters on bases here in Mass. It is next to impossible to get onto a fire department in Massachusetts. Your best shot is on your hometown fire department. Also it's who you know. We don't know anyone! But Mike is driven and determined to become a firefighter when he returns home. He e mails fire chiefs from different towns to see if they are hiring anytime in the future. They are all very kind to respond and thank him for his service, but advise him to try to get onto the dept in his hometown.

12/20/06

Going to finish grading my fire exams. Not too happy with the first 15 so far. But I know with actually firefighting shit I'm good. It would be nice if handscom was hiring so I could use all of my certs but whatever. Gotta go, love mike.

12/24/06

Well I wanna say Merry Xmas now cause I don't know what will be up with the phones or anything, so who knows. So merry xmas everyone.

12/25/06 - Christmas day.

We did not hear from Mike today. Merry Christmas

1/1/07

Hey what's up, I didn't do anything for new years, I had it as my day off, we have to wear our flak and Kevlar everywhere now and it's hot. We got bombed towards the night so it made it more interesting, and that's about all I did.

Oh, lovely. He got bombed last night. So I went to work and say hello to everyone and I want to scream, "Hey, someone please listen to me and understand what I'm going through", my son was bombed last night, he could have died. He could die everyday, do you people understand". But instead, my conversation goes something like this. "Hi, how are you. Thanks I'm fine." Then I begin my day. I hold it all in. But I want to scream.

1/1/07

If I calculated it right, then I might be home by June 27th, that's if I decide not to take any leave in Cali.

1/11/07

Hey what's Up, I'm alright. We lost internet and phones and shit cause we lost guys, but we are back now. I love you guys. Had to come work on my day off, so I can't call you guys today. My back is going to explode, I had the best workout even considering I had to go by myself and we can only go at night now alone so it fucking blows. I'm going to be huge for the United States.

1/14/07

Hi Mike,

Its dad. I just go through talking to the head of the Worcester firefighters union. He gave me a few suggestions for you.

1/22/07

Hey busy here. I'm driving around in a huge armored 7 ton in the surrounding towns guarding fucking Iraqi's doing work so I'll be busy next couple of days.

Hi Mike,

Don't like that, roadside bombs and all. Please, please be careful.

I love you, love mom

1/22/07

Mom, its cool, it's a bad ass truck and trust me it's armored to hell. And it's only the town like right outside of base. It's fine I got all my gear and everything and trust me I'll shoot one of the fuckers if they try shit. Ha ha.

Eileen Gelsomini

1/29/07

Right now there is a windstorm type of thing and it sucks. I wanna go fishing; catch some turtles or maybe some bass and a nice cigar. Love mike

1/30/07

Hey when u guys are in Cali waiting for my plane to come in have a pizza ready for me ha ha.

Mike seems to be in much better spirits with this deployment. I know its not what he's doing, or what he's seen, because its about the same as last time, maybe even a little more, but I think it's the fact that his 4 years are coming to an end and he knows this is the last time he will be going to Iraq. He's talking about his homecoming and it isn't for another three months or so, but if that's what it takes to keep him going, well then, great.

It is late at night and we receive a phone call from Mike, It's about 2am and the ringing startles us out of sleep. I can't say deep sleep, because we haven't had that in three years.

But nonetheless, it's jolting. He doesn't sound too upbeat. He sounds a little depressed. Maybe because he is homesick. John runs to the kitchen phone as he always does when Mike calls. Our conversation is sparse. For some reason, we don't know what to say to him. How is everything? What are you doing? Things like that, and my son isn't a "talker" anyway over the phone, so the conversation is strained. John and I are still half asleep. John brought up fishing and baseball and it seems to snap him out of his funk. I just listen, content to hear my sons voice. Suddenly, we hear something, not sure what it is and then the phone went dead. John and I swear we heard the words "incoming". But we are not sure. On this particular base, they seemed to be getting mortared quite a bit. Mike doesn't call back. John and I wonder what happened. We are worried sick.

Another sleepless night – I went downstairs to e mail him to see if everything was ok.

We hear from Mike in an e mail, that everything is fine. He informs me that they don't say "incoming". I guess I watched too many episode of Mash. But that's what it sounded like. Mike said, the phone lines just went dead. My nerves are frazzled and I can't shake the feeling that something is going to happen this deployment.

2/4/7

Hey what's up? Same shit here. Bored Sunday. We got hit yesterday. Yea like 20 feet from where I sit and work. Pretty crazy. It blew our gunnies windows out and our door off. So yea not a good way to end the day, but whatever, no biggy. Love mike.

Hey, well I can't really tell you in e mail and shit exactly what I'm doing but now I'm in a 7 ton for the most part and the rest I'm outside guarding them. I have no motivation anymore in the gym. I don't know what happened. I think it is because it's always full when we go so it's a slow workout. Love mike

We carry on as usual. I noticed now, that just my immediate family asks about Mike, and no one else. It's like the war is over for everyone. Only a few of my co-workers ask how Mike is doing or how I am doing. And just a handful of clients. People can't relate. If my son had cancer, then people would ask how he is or how I am. Because almost everyone can relate to that. Everyone either knows someone who had it or at least can fathom the idea of being sick. My co-worker's father has cancer. He is terminal. I feel bad for my co-worker. Her father is about 80 and so I think of my own parent's mortality. How they will finally go. I hope it isn't cancer. She is going thru a tough time and limits her work hours to visit her father and tend to her mother's needs. It takes approximately 4 months for her father to die. During that time, we treat her with "kid gloves". If she is moody or upset, we realize that she is going thru a tough time. Since I work at a Spa, a few people decide to treat her by surprising her and give her a "day of beauty" which consists of a massage, facial, manicure, the works. She does need it and that is so typically kind of my co-workers.

If I sound the least bit resentful or jealous, that would be accurate. I am. I feel like the worse person in the world for thinking this way. The love you have for a parent, sibling, relative or a friend is so different from the love you have for your child. I think to myself, if I lost my job, and my house caught on fire and God forbid one of my parents had cancer, all at the same time...it wouldn't even be close to the feeling of waking up every day wondering if your child is dead or alive and in harms way every single day or heaven forbid to die. Not to downplay a fire or losing your job or cancer. Any one, those things are devastating, but...something happening to your child and it doesn't matter the age, that's incomprehensible. My heart goes out to anyone whose child is very sick, or had died.

I told my friend, Eileen, in the very beginning that if anything ever happened to Michael over in Iraq, that she was to be at my side and help me to receive counseling. She was not to ever leave me alone because the only thing that would keep me alive would be my other two children. My husband would understand. Thinking about this sounds morbid, but I do think it, often.

So while I am sympathetic to my co-worker, I want to say to everyone "what about me"... do any of you have any idea what I am going through every single day of my son's deployment?. Do any of you who have children comprehend this? Of course I don't say this and feel extremely bad for even thinking this way. I guess my whole point here is what I've known from the "get go", that the only person who understands is my husband. I'll end this "pity party" I'm having for myself now.

Eileen Gelsomini

It is different for John, he gets asks often from his co-workers and his sub-contractors. In fact most people he meets weekly. It must be a guy thing, he tells me. You know, Marines, war, etc. He talks politics with everyone he meets. He has intelligent conversations. Ok, arguments sometimes as we are staunch Republicans and most people he meets are Democrats. This is Massachusetts after all. But I envy him. I am very involved in politics, we both watch at least 5 hours of news everyday. There is only one co-worker, that I can talk politics with. And all and I mean all of my clients are Democrats.

It amazes me that for some reason my clients will be in my room and feel it either necessary to speak their mind about the war or politics. They just assume that I am as angry as they are about the war. I never and I mean never bring up politics. I thought that was a given. Unless of course you both had the same views. So I am in a predicament when this happens. Do I act professional like I am supposed to and ignore them and change the subject? Do I listen to their anger and rant about our President and his policies and pretend to agree with them so I don't lose them as clients? I admit, I have ignored most people. However, their have been times when they do reference certain policies that I have to respond. I'll say this, after I have said my viewpoint, the look on their face is pure amazement. I guess they assume that I hate this administration because my son is over in Iraq. I don't know why. I want to tell them that, not only was I a conservative before my son entered the Marine Corps, but that because he is fighting for this country, (and yes, I do believe he is fighting to preserve this countries' freedom), that my views have deepened these past four years. My husband and I have constantly switched TV news to see how other stations are reporting the news. When I knew for a fact that for instance the surge was working over in Iraq, only one news station reported that. What a slap in the face for our military. Most people who have the yellow stickers on their car really should take them off. Because how can you support the military but be against the war. Now I know that people say you can do both. I disagree. Obviously no one wants our men and women in uniform to be hurt or worse to die. But I look at it this way…it would be like your son going to a college that you don't agree with, don't agree with his major of study and voice it often and with anger, tell him he is going to fail and should just come home, but then turning around in the same breath and tell him you support him. That to me sends mixed signals. I want to tell people, if you don't believe in the same cause the troops believe in, want them to come home and say we will not win, well then you really don't support them. You may hope they don't get hurt, but support them I don't think so. We need a different word on those yellow stickers. This may be a simplistic comparison, but it's how I feel.

John usually takes the same route home from work. He began to notice a man holding a sign on the side of a pretty busy street. The sign said, "Impeach the Lying Bastard".

Ok, again, first amendment. Freedom of speech is what this country is most proud of.

However, we are at a time of war, and I believe that everyone who speaks out should at least have the decency to do it respectfully. John decided to make a sign of his own. I never thought for one minute that he wouldn't do it. On his way home from work whenever he saw this man holding that sign, he would park his car and stand right next to him. His sign said simply "Support our President". At first John and this man had words, going at it back and forth. By the second or third time, it became a peaceful protest; both tolerating each other's presence. Finally the man moved across the street. I think John was taking away some of his attention, which is why I think he had that sign anyway. This lasted about 4 weeks. Whenever John would see him, he would call me on his cell and say to me "I'm going to be a little late for dinner tonight". And I knew just where he was.

CHAPTER 13
Countdown

Stephanie and I are home. It is later on in the afternoon. It is starting to get dark outside. I'm in my living room and our dog Chucky is on our couch looking out the window as he always does. His ears go up and he starts to bark. I look outside to see what he is barking at. I notice a car that went up the street very slowly. I can't really see who is inside. I live at the beginning of a cul-de-sac. The car passes my house and turns around. It starts to come back again. Then it pulled over across the street a house down from me. Now the car is just sitting there. It looked like a government vehicle very non-descript. I feel panic start to rise up inside. I don't say a word to Stephanie. The car turned around and parked in front of my house. I still can't see inside. My heart starts to race. Oh my God, this can't be happening. Please God, don't make this be the military coming to my house. When your son is over in Iraq, the last thing you want to see is a military car pull up to your home. I'm so panicked that I can't say a word, can't react. Should I go outside to see who it is and what they want? I feel dizzy, like I'm going to pass out. I feel like throwing up. This can't be happening. After what seems like 45 minutes, but in reality about 10 minutes, I call Stephanie over. We both stare out the window for 5 minutes. What is going on, why is the car just sitting there? They are probably verifying the address and gaining their composure before knocking on my door and giving me the dreadful news that my son was killed in action.

I'm almost ready to have a panic attack and lose it, when Stephanie said to me. "I know that car, that's Mr. Raeke's car". (Mr. Raeke is the driver Ed instructor for Hudson High School). I ask, "Are you sure?" She is, she recognizes it. Just then the car starts to pull away and drive off. On the back we see, "Student Driver".

My eyes fill up. Relief is not strong enough to describe what I just felt.

I gain another 50 gray hairs. I call John and told him what happened. I feel like I just lost 2 years of my life with that incident. I felt like God just spared my son. Immediately I think of how those other mothers must have felt when the same thing happened to them, but only for them, it was a Military vehicle. I say a prayer and thank God. I say another one and pray for all the families

Courage & Faith

who have lost their loved ones. I manage to miss this one. For now anyway, Mike is safe.

We are starting a count down for Mike's arrival in April. Like before we can't make plane reservations yet until the last moment. I let them know at work, that my notice will be within a week's timeframe. I can't give them anymore notice than that. But my clients won't mind the last minute cancellation. My good clients all know Mike is over in Iraq and I may have to cancel their appointments. They are understanding and excited for me.

Over the last few months, Mike has asked me to send his resume out. He has limited access to the computer and when he does have time, someone else is on it and he misses a chance, or there is a time limit. I send his resume out on his behalf to most every town. I receive emails from the chiefs asking me to thank my son for his service. They all let me know that his best chance of becoming a firefighter is within his own town of Hudson.

The way the civil service of Massachusetts works is that you take the civil service test. You receive about 2 extra points for being a veteran. Then you are placed in the first category of veterans before the residents, but only in your home town. Every other town he ranks near the bottom because the residents of that specific town come first.

There are also points awarded for firefighting experience. I print out the form and it says that only firefighters in towns and municipalities are given credit for firefighting experience. I e mail the civil service commission and ask if my son who is a Firefighter in the Marine Corps. will received these extra points. Michael went thru firefighting academy that met Mass. Standards. He is firefighter I, II and airport firefighter certified. He is Hazmat Certified, first responder certified, Emergency Vehicle Operations Certified and American Heart Certified. He has put out fires, both structural and aircraft, he has pulled dead bodies out of planes and helo's. He has probably seen more death than the average town firefighter at his age. I am told simply that No, he will not receive the 2 points extra for this as he was not a firefighter in a "town or city". They do not count Military firefighter experience. Period. upport the troops my ass. Thank you Massachusetts.

Being the worrier that I am, I begin to think about Michael's future. What will it hold?

When I look up the Fire Department in Hudson, it is quite full and has quite a few on call firefighters as well. How long will it take Michael to become a firefighter? I am told by many fire chiefs that people wait normally 5 to 10 years to get onto a department and most people just never get on.

What will Michael do when he comes home? I voice this to John. John tells me that Mike will figure it out. What does he mean Mike will figure it out. He needs a second plan just in case. In this day and age most young people need college or a technical degree. Mike has neither. I'm worried, John is not. It has nothing to

Courage & Faith

do with having faith in your child, and everything to do with the difference in our personalities. I'm a worrier, John is not. This aggravates me. It annoys me because he should worry a little at least and annoys me because I can't be like that, can't let it go.

Just for a second I think about if Mike attended college and never went into the Marine Corps. But then, I would have never gotten so involved in politics, something I found out I enjoy. I would have never had the opportunity to go to Parris Island, never had the opportunity to have the absolute joy of seeing your only son walk down the stairs of a plane bringing him home from Iraq. Never appreciated the Pledge of Allegiance and have it truly mean something, not that it didn't before, but knowing that you temporarily gave your son to this country. The words have a whole different meaning. So for the four years of (not to sound dramatic here), but four years of hell and joy this has been, I honestly do not regret my son joining the Marine Corp. I wouldn't trade these four years for all the tea in china. And I am sorry for all the parents out there that do not have this experience.

On that note, I am enclosing a letter that I wrote to the Metrowest Daily Newspaper in the editorial section. Every day my husband and I would look at the "Letters to the Editor" section. There was one letter in particular that I had to respond to. It was from a woman who was outraged that at her son's high school college fair, there was a Military recruiting table. She advised all parents to go onto the website

"Leavemychildalone.org.".

Here is my letter to that woman and many like her.

JOIN MILITARY WITH PRIDE.

Regarding the letter to the editor "Military School Invasion" in the Sept 3 MetroWest Daily News and the Website www.leavemychildalone.org. It's too bad that most American parents would rather not have their child even consider the option of serving their country. This kind of mentality has been around a very long time, especially in the Northeast. Everyone wants their country protected and everyone agrees that we need a military force, just as long as it doesn't involve their child. I wish this country would make it mandatory for all high school graduates to serve their country proudly for a year or two. I can guarantee that when their child was through, he would be a much more self sufficient and mature person than had he not served and know that this is the greatest country on earth. They would learn honor, courage, sacrifice and commitment. I know this firsthand as my son who is a United States Marine and recently returned from Iraq has the "never give up" attitude that served him well with the Crash/Fire/Rescue Unit now, and hopefully as a future firefighter for Massachusetts.

Eileen Gelsomini- Hudson

This newspaper and many like it across the country were outraged at the treatment of the prisoners at Abu Graib prison. They painted American Soldiers in a very bad light.

Eileen Gelsomini

Many letters to the editor from average citizens also wrote with their outrage.

The following is a letter to the editor I wrote to the MetroWest Daily News.

This one is in regard to the Two American Soldiers kidnapped and tortured and killed by terrorist. Not one newspaper reported this on the front page. If not at all, then it was on the 15th page. A tiny article that no one would see. If that had been two American Soldiers doing the torturing, well then, it would be all over the front page of every newspaper, on every news station, just how bad and depraved our Soldiers are. Well where is the outrage for OUR Soldiers? Why isn't anyone upset? I looked at the front page of our newspaper and saw nothing on this. Two of America's Bravest kidnapped, heads cut off, etc found in a ditch and not one mention. Why? Because the media does not want anyone to know. Period. That would mean telling it like it is, that the terrorist we are fighting, you know the ones that crashed into the world trade center and took three of our planes down along with innocent men, women and children, those terrorist are really out there and are really the bad guys.

Instead the papers focused on Abu Graib prison and how bad America is, how we could let a soldier hold a barking German Shepard close to a Terrorist (who probably was responsible for killing our American soldiers/Marines.)

Here is my letter to the Editor.

Courage & Faith

DOESN'T ANYONE CARE?

Two United States soldiers were taken by force a few days ago in Iraq. I spent the last few days praying that the 8,000 soldiers and Marines would find them. Well, they did find them, lying in a field booby-trapped with explosive devices to make their bodies harder to reach.

The two young men were tortured beyond belief. Beheaded, body parts cut off and stuffed in their mouths, hacked up barely beyond recognition. Geneva Convention rules don't apply to the terrorist. I expected to open the paper today and see this somewhere on the front page because we as Americans should be so outraged by this. It wasn't. Yet when American military hold a barking dog too close for comfort to a prisoner or a soldier points at a prisoner's genitals and humiliates them at Abu Ghraib, its all over the front pages of every newspaper and media for months on end.

Could the MetroWest Daily news have at least put this story about our soldiers in place of the Fluffernutter sandwich story on the bottom right corner? I mean, I know the press and media are run by liberals and so this is just not as important to them as someone else from another country being tortured (see example above), but can you throw a bone to the rest of us who do care once in a while?

Eileen and John Gelsomini

Later that day, I received a call from a Framingham, Ma Firefighter whose son just came home from the Marine Corp. He thanked me for writing that letter and said he spoke for the entire Framingham Fire Department.

That made my day. In the months to come John and I cancelled out subscription to our local newspaper.

2/06/07

We haven't heard from Mike in a while. We're getting worried. One would think we would get used to this especially being his second deployment, but it doesn't work that way. We e mailed Mike to see if he would respond and let us know he was OK

Finally an email

Hey we were in river city so we had no phones or email. We have a lot of projects going on this week and with the airfield and shit so we'll be busy a lot. Love mike

He wrote this on a few occasions – I'm referring to him being in River City. I wonder where River City is. I punch it up on Google. I look at the map hanging on our refrigerator. I can't find River City. What is he doing there?

I mention this to Lori and she said that when Mike says they were in River City, That means simply that all communication is down for whatever reason, usually security reasons or that Marines have died and they don't want word to leak out before they tell the families. River city is the code phrase.

I feel like an idiot. Here I am looking for River City on the map, telling everyone how my son is in River City, maybe on a dangerous mission. I thought I was familiar with all the Marine Corp terms and slang, but I haven't even skimmed the surface.

Well I am relieved at any rate.

We receive an email from Mike. He wants me to have the Navy Unit Commendation award added to his resume. We look up what exactly the Navy Unit Commendation Award is. (Outstanding Achievement in a Deployed unit) it said something about combat mission, but Mike told me to leave that out on his resume.

We are so proud of him.

Mike's next few emails are all about his homecoming and when he is discharged from the Marine Corp altogether. I think that is what keeps him going out there and keeps his spirits up. He talks of going fishing, driving his truck in the snow, getting a boat, and going to the Red Sox games. I think that because he has strong family ties and is grounded that he'll be Ok mentally when he comes home. If I had fears the last homecoming, I don't have them with this deployment. I feel bad for all the young military men and women who do not have the same family situation awaiting them when they are discharged. I'm glad we have provided Mike with such stability and know that he knows how lucky he is.

Hey yea, I almost died , ha ha, I just go out of the showers and right when I came up we got hit with mortars, Yeah they hit the trailers I was in. Fuck man I was going to shave too and I would have been a little longer. That's the second time in a row they hit near our building. They know our positions. Fun, fun. Well igtg love mike

2/21/07

We read that email. Is this ever going to end? Wished he didn't tell us that. I guess he thought it was Ok, because he was all right. That night, John's mother who had been in the hospital since yesterday, died. We emailed Mike to let him know.

2/22/07

I'm so sorry dad It sucks being over here because there isn't anything that I can do. It fucking sucks so much. I'm not really in the mood anymore to write a long email cause this really sucks bad. I just wanted to say I'm sorry dad. Sorry about the email, telling you guys about what almost happened to me last night. Bad timing and you didn't need to here it. I hope you guys at home are doing somewhat alright.
Love always. Mike

Mike had asked Lori to attend the wake and funeral on his behalf. I think that this deployment coupled with his mother dying is getting to John. This was the last straw, we need Mike home. I went to work the next day. When I entered the spa for some reason I simply just lost my composure in front of the spa manager. I think John's mother dying just added to everything and it got to be too much. I went home and took off the next 4 days. We had much to do. John's father passed some 9 years before and we had her house to deal with. Getting it ready to sell was a job and a half, but kept us busy and focused on something other than Mike for the most part.

2/25/07

Hey just got in from burning a bunch of classified shit. Smoked one of the cigars Lori sent me. It was alright. It's a great day out so just chilled out there. Remind me of fishing, ha ha. I can't fucking wait to go fishing again. Well letting you guys know I'm alright.

2/2/407

Shitty day just go back from the gym. And I guess this country is so fucked up they like to bomb each other so the bombed the town like a mile from us and now it's a big mass casualty thing here on base cause we are bringing them all to our surgical. There are tons of blown up kids and shit like old people and like tons of them and we are helping with that so that was fucked up to see. So all in all a shitty day. There's way too much death this whole deployment. Love me

I'm wondering if Mike will make it home alive. We've come this far, we are so close to seeing him. I can't even talk to anyone anymore. I sound like a broken record. Mike's base was mortared; if he had made the decision to shave he would have been dead. That's the reality of it. That Mike came minutes from death. Try to comprehend that and then go to work and act normal around people. What a joke.

With every day, I pray nothing happens. This is all I want out of life, my son safely home.

The next few weeks were spent with e mails back and forth regarding information on his homecoming. Mid March was the target date with again a few days here or there.

CHAPTER 14
Second Homecoming

It is my last day of work before heading out to California. I have so much energy I could literally run home instead of taking my car.

John and I are again headed to San Diego. If I never see San Diego again, it'll be too soon! We bring our sign, the one we made the first time, our Welcome Home sign. We are pro's at this we think to ourselves and head to our hotel. After we unpack John and I head directly to the Base. "That plane better be arriving on time", John said to me. I agree. I am not going to go through what I did the last time. When we arrive at the hanger and look at the flight board, we indeed see that his plane will arrive Tuesday afternoon. Tomorrow John and I will walk around a little, grab some lunch and hope our nerves don't get the best of us. Mike's Marine Corp career is coming to a close. Yahoo. We'll have our son home in no time.

Eileen Gelsomini

Tuesday Morning.

John and I head to Miramar Air Base. Mike's arrival time is changed a little. Now it is due at 3pm. I look at John, he looks at me. Not again. This time, we don't leave for lunch, we have no appetite. Families start to pile in. We strike up a conversation with a mother and daughter. Turns out she has heard all about "Gelso" from her son. Gelso is Mike's nickname. And as it turns out John's nickname when he was Mike's age as well. No surprise there, not with a last name like Gelsomini. We speak of the last 7 months of this deployment and have so many similarities.

John decided to get up and look at the flight board again. This time the arrival has moved once again to 7pm. Great I think, it's going to be dark outside and we won't be able to see a thing. That plane had better land at 7pm.

I grab a snack that is on the table provided for the families. John just wants water. I wonder if Mike was serious when he asked us to have a pizza waiting for him on his arrival. 6:30pm approaches and a woman in uniform informs us that the plane is 15 minutes away. She caught me off guard for some reason and I panic to get to the side door as fast as I could. I left John a few people behind me. He'll catch up.

The crowd gathers, 200 strong. This time, they have a band which starts to play patriotic music. TV cameras are also there. If the sound of a band playing Marine Corp songs doesn't bring you to tears at your son's homecoming, then you had better check your pulse.

This time, John saw the plane and almost without much warning, it swooped down before us just like before. I know the drill now, the plane creeps up the runway to turn around.

This takes about 40 minutes. 40 agonizing minutes. Ok, here they come, the crowd cheers and whistles. We wait again for the door to open and the Marines to file out.

One by one, slowly they file out. Then it seems all at once, hundreds descend on the tarmac. John is scanning for Mike. I am crying, the band is still playing. I feel extremely lucky to be right where I am at that moment. John cannot find Mike this time and hope Mike sees us. We are holding up the sign, but decide it is a waste because it is dusk. After a brief speech by the company commander, the crowd breaks free and everyone scurries to find their loved ones.

It didn't take long this time, because Mike found us. We hugged him like never before. He did it. He escaped being hurt or worse. Done, finished. We found his friend Josh and proceeded to gather their sea bags and turn in their rifles. Mike told us that they didn't need to do anything else that night. Tomorrow they would get their trucks and get all their belongings out of storage for their new rooms.

The next few days went by in a blur of meals, and attending to all of Mike's and Josh's needs. It felt so good to know that this would be the last time I would have to go through all of this.

It was time for John and me to leave once more. This time for good. It wasn't half bad at all – the good-bye. I knew that it would only be a matter of months before Mike would be home to us.

CHAPTER 15
Preparing For Civilian Life

spring/summer 2008

Spring is finally here, the weather is getting warmer. One night John and I had my daughter, Valerie and her husband Dave over. Valerie looked up at me and told me she is going to the doctor for her second checkup. Checkup? What kind of checkup? She smiles and lets me know that she is pregnant. We are overjoyed. I am going to be a grandmother. At 48!! It is to be a Christmas Baby, due December 26th. I can't believe it. Within ten minutes Val and I are shopping. I buy her some maternity outfits. This will be the best Christmas ever, my entire family, plus our brand new grandchild!!

It is the beginning of May. One more month and Mike will be home forever. On Mother's Day we all went to brunch my daughter Val and her husband Dave and my daughter Stephanie. Valerie called my parents in Florida to tell them the good news. They will be great grandparents. Life was getting better all the time.

The next day, Monday morning, my phone rang. As soon as she said, "Mom'. I knew by the sound of her voice. No heartbeat she cried over the phone. The baby died a few days ago. She was inconsolable.

The next day I start to spring clean Mike's room. We purchase a new mattress for Mike, new curtains and comforter. Things he has not had for four years. Our dog of 12 ½ years Chucky slept in Mike's bed the entire four years. It was not Mike's room, it was Chuckys own bedroom. I like to think that Chucky did that because he missed Mike, which I know he did. But in reality he slept on Mike's bed simply because he was the most spoiled dog in America. We wondered what he'll do once Mike occupied that room. I couldn't wait to see the reunion between Mike and Chucky. One day in May we took Chucky to the vet for his annual rabies shot. On the ride home Chucky got violently ill. Back to the vet he went the next day and had some tests. A day later it was confirmed. Chucky had cancer. Lung cancer to be exact.

The news hit us hard. Like every family who loves their dog, Chucky was a huge part of our life. One we couldn't imagine without him. How much longer, we asked the vet? "Oh, about 8 months or so, hard to say".

Courage & Faith

Just treat him well, give him steak often, and someday when he is in pain, you'll know it's getting close. So we figured Chucky would hopefully make it until at least Christmas. Just let Mike enjoy him for a few more months after he is home.

Everyday Chucky seemed to be getting worse. We hoped that he would make it at least until the end of June so Mike could say good-bye. We did not want the agonizing decision to put him to sleep. We hoped that Chucky would die with us in our home, so we could bury him outside. Every day he seemed to be losing more and more energy. Until one day a few weeks from his diagnosis my daughter Valerie came over to see him. Now Chucky was loved by all of us, but he was Val's dog. I think she loved him the most. That evening Chucky was full of energy and played with Val like he was a puppy. We couldn't believe it, maybe it wasn't cancer, and maybe he had a virus. He was jumping and playing with Val. No way was this dog that sick. Chucky died the next morning.

I received a call from a very distraught Stephanie. John came home right away. We got our wish, he died in our house. I guess the evening with Val was his way of saying to all of us "please remember me this way". He is buried in our backyard with a cross, his collar and leash. We buried him with a hotdog (he ate them often) and a dog bone and his favorite toy. Mike never got the chance to say good-by. We love you Chuck!

We started the countdown for Mike's homecoming. This has not been a great year. Mike in Iraq, John's mother passing away Valerie's miscarriage and our beloved Chucky gone. To say our nerves were shot would be an understatement. But now we are focusing on the future. It can only get better.

So to the airport we all went for one final time. It felt good. We of course arrived earlier than we should have which made the waiting seem all the more drawn out. Every few minutes we would check the board to see if his plane landed. When it finally did, we all got to our feet and waited until we saw him walk through those doors to us. To anybody watching us, we looked just like another family waiting for someone to come home from a vacation or whatnot. No one could ever tell just what a special homecoming this was. They couldn't possibly know the worry we have had these past 4 years and how this was the culmination of his military career. John kept looking at the flight board to see when Mike's plane finally landed. He looked at me and smiled. My son was home. Mike finally did walk past those double doors to us, right into our waiting arms so we could all give him a hug. The only evidence to strangers that he was in the military would be his bald head and his Marine Corp camouflage backpack that he wore. But to me, the evidence was a lot clearer. I did not need the Marine Corp Logo on his duffle bag, nor the backpack he wore to know that he was a Marine. It was evident in his walk.

John carried his duffle bag which must have weighed 100 pounds. I think John would have carried my son if he could, all the way to the car. I watched as my husband and son walked side by side ahead of me to our car. Tears filled my eyes.

We all had no idea what the future would hold for Mike. Would he find a job right away? What kind of job would that be? How long would it take him to get onto a fire department? Would that ever happen at all given the percentage of people that actually make it?

For now, though, I'll put those worried aside, even if just for a little bit. Mike was tired, but talked through the entire ride home. I wonder what is going through Mike's mind when we finally pulled up to the house that night from the airport. Is it relief? Is it uncertainty? Does he wonder how he will begin to fit in into Civilian life? All of the above I suspect. But when we pull into our driveway and start to unload his things, I just see Mike with a slight smile almost like he just got back from vacation, glad to be home and I suspect just plain tired. The first thing we all do is walk with Mike to Chucky's grave out in the backyard. After that somber moment we head inside.

The next morning I stare at Mike at breakfast. It seems weird for him to occupy his bedroom and to have him for dinner every night. At first, he catches up with his friends, and makes the rounds. He seems happy to be home naturally if only just a little restless. He probably feels a little bit without a purpose right now. Since Mike isn't officially out of the Marine Corps until August (with 3 more years considered inactive reserve), he does have a paycheck for the next 8 weeks. So Mike spends every moment doing what he only dreamt about the last four years. Eating when he wants, sleeping when he wants, growing a beard and going fishing.

One Sunday, I watch as Mike and John pull out of the driveway, fishing poles in the backseat of the Jeep Wrangler, top off, doors off and head out to one of their many fishing spots. All I see are two bald heads from the back. I smile and tear up a bit. My husband has his son home. John has waited for this moment for four long years.

CHAPTER 16
Civilian Life

Fall approaches and Mike begins to look for a job in earnest. Again, I worry. He takes the military makeup civil service test. Mike in the meantime went down to the Hudson Fire Station. The chief let him know that their will be an opening on the department soon and to let him know when he receives his score and hopefully he'll be at the top of the list. When the Civil Service Score envelope arrived in the mail, Mike is apprehensive to open it. Mike received a good score and when he looked on the civil service website at the list for Hudson, we learn he placed number One. I believe that day he called the chief. We later learned that the opening was for the On Call position, not a permanent full time position. So Mike is placed on the On Call List. He is number 15, the last person on the list. He is informed that it will take approximately 10 years give or take for a position to open up and to perhaps get onto the department full time. But no guarantees either. Things do not look so great, but if on call is all there is, well then Mike has to take that.

Michael does find employment with a construction company. It will be good hands on learning experience for him, John tells me. I agree. At least when he has his own home, he will know how to repair things. The pay is low, but Mike is used to that. He is living at home and will be able to pay his bills, but that is about it. Still, I can't help being disappointed that it is so hard for Mike to get onto a fire department. I hope my son doesn't see this, as I try to hide it. I voice it to John often. I'm not disappointed in my son of course; I am disappointed at the "system". Being a veteran doesn't give Mike many advantages as one thinks it does. He places at the bottom of the other three towns he has listed on the civil service test as he is not a resident. Now what? Now we wait. For what, I don't know and that's the problem. I don't "wait" well. I'm impatient by nature and I don't take "No" for an answer very well either. But I have no choice. He may have to work in construction or whatever for years my husband tells me and so I should just get used to it. Mike will find his own way. Massachusetts does have a coming home bonus for Veterans and Mike takes advantage of this. He definitely could use the money. Now and again an add in the paper will turn up a firefighter position. All of them however want an EMT license.

Mike applied for a firefighter position he found on line. He received an email later on that day telling him to contact them when he does have an EMT license. This scenario plays out several times in the next year. Near misses for a firefighter position.

Mike does enroll in an EMT class that will take him four months at night to complete. I know how much he hates going to school and for someone else, 4 months is nothing, but for Mike, it is a long time. He has to do this, he knows if there is any chance whatsoever in becoming a firefighter. He would take any firefighter job in any town in Mass. Anyone who wants to become a firefighter in this state feels the same way. He would love to have a chance at a firefighter position on one of our military bases in the state or Massport (Logan Airport Fire Department). But again, these positions are hard to come by.

John has many contacts in the "firefighting world". Most firefighters have second jobs and John knows quite a few in the construction business. They are all so helpful in giving advice to us. Many have said to John that if something opens up somewhere, they will do whatever they can to put in a good word for Mike. We thank them all. In the meantime, Mike received an e mail that he picked up Sergeant in the Marine Corps. Something he wanted to achieve before he officially left the Corps.

It is September and the weather is beautiful as it typically is in New England this time of year. Valerie came over and we were having a nice mother daughter afternoon on my deck when she whispers, don't tell anyone yet, but I am pregnant again. They want to wait a few more weeks to let everyone know. I feel privileged to know this information before anyone. I am overjoyed again. And when she leaves later on that day, I whisper to John that he is going to be a grandfather. Please don't let anyone know that I told you, I say to him. Another few weeks go by and I receive a phone call. I was by myself on Monday and Valerie tearfully lets me know that she lost the baby again. I tell her to come over as soon as she can. Come on, God, can you please throw us a bone here. Haven't we had enough drama for these past four years? Val and I spend an afternoon in peace with her lying on my couch, still miscarrying. I wish I had a bottle of wine.

It was Christmastime and I was feeling a little melancholy thinking about Valerie and Dave and how they must feel. I would have had my grandchild this month. How I wished Chucky was here for one last Christmas. It wasn't meant to be. I poured myself a glass of wine. I should get myself into a better place mentally. John was sitting on the couch watching TV. A commercial came on the screen. There is sad music playing in the background. It's a commercial for abandoned dogs. You can probably guess where this one is going.

We named her Mia. She was half Daschund and half Jack Russell; all eight pounds of her. We didn't want a larger dog that resembled Chucky. And as much as I was

Courage & Faith

starting to enjoy my freedom, I did miss having a dog. I did have mixed feelings at first and I admit wanted to give her back, but too late. John and Mike already loved this puppy.

Christmas was approaching and I was getting into the spirit. This is what I have been waiting for; my entire family here with us. My shopping was finished, parties were planned. It was a Tuesday 2 weeks before Christmas, December 11th. Many mothers just know when something is wrong with their children. I believe that mothers have a kind of ESP or instinct unlike fathers for some reason. I consider myself to have this power pretty strong when it comes to a lot of things, but especially involving my children. I had that feeling as soon as I entered my house. My daughter who was home on Winter break from college had left the house in a rush. There was a half eaten bagel on the table. I quickly took out my cell phone and noticed 17 missed calls. This can't be good. When I listen to voicemail, it is John and it simply said to call him. You know the news can't be good when a person can't say what it is on the phone. John picked up and he told me that the Gas Company blew up Val and Dave's house. The house that John and Val and Dave and countless others spent their blood, sweat and tears renovating before they were married. What do you mean, "Blew up". Blew Up, leveled, the only thing left standing was the staircase. Watching it on the news that night seems surreal. Val and Dave came over that night and spent the next month living with us. Weeks went by and upon investigation, it turns out that the gas company was negligent and punctured a gas line. Thankfully no one was home. But they lost everything, wedding pictures, family heirlooms, all their possessions. They had two cats. One of the cats made it out and when the firefighter caught her, she was on fire, but alive. The other cat wasn't so lucky. Days passed and Dave and Val started to sift threw their charred belongings. Valerie thought she heard a faint mewing. Dave told her it must be wishful thinking. Later on that day, Valerie was in the bank where everyone knew her and what had happened. Her cell phone rang and a neighbor found her other cat buried, but relatively Ok trapped under some debris in their yard. That made Valerie's day needless to say.

Valerie and Dave have had a lot of losses in 2007, her two miscarriages, John's mother, her beloved Dog, and now their home. We found out that the gas company is not liable for the damage they caused to the home. Their chances for any legal action is limited in Massachusetts because they did not witness the accident or were not injured, therefore the law states that they have no stress related to the explosion.

I pray that 2008 is a better year for the Gelsomini's and Fitzgerald's.

CHAPTER 17
What the Future Holds

It's been a year now since Mike has been home. I think he is fully adjusted to civilian life, but I do think it took him a good while. He is still disciplined in working out, and eating healthy. He still cleans his room weekly. There are a few leftover nuances from his military life hanging around. None are alarming, however and this I am thankful for. There is still a can of Febreeze in his bedroom; he still uses a wet mop on his bedroom floor. Leftover traits from his inspection days. One thing John and I notice is that Mike hardly ever speaks of his military days, good or bad. I think he has referenced a handful of incidents since he has been home. But these only pertain to San Diego. He has never disclosed to John or myself what he had done or seen over in Iraq. And truth be told, I don't want to know. Ever. My family on occasion have asked me if Mike has ever spoke of Iraq or told us anything. I'm not sure why they want to hear details. I think it's probably human nature to hear gory details about things, but I always tell them the same answer. Mike never speaks of Iraq. My mother has mentioned to me that maybe he is keeping everything inside and that it would be good for Mike to let it out, to tell someone. I see her point. Much in the way that a person who has gone through a horrific experience needs to tells a therapist or someone that has gone through the same thing. But maybe that's just it. I am neither a therapist nor have I seen war. Maybe he has had that conversation with his Military friends. Maybe he needs to sort that out himself. Maybe he never will speak about that part of his life and prefers to keep it that way. John has a few times asked Mike very simple "leading" questions, but Mike always gave him a vague answer. And so we leave it at that. I am content for now seeing my son make his way back into civilian life. I see him happy and productive. He has interests, hobbies, and friends. Most important, he has us, his family who love him unconditionally. And when and if he is ready to unload someday, we will be there. Hopefully, someday he will have a wife and family and the memories will fade somewhat. But no, Mike does not mention his deployments. He hardly mentions San Diego. Sometimes I think I have Post Traumatic Stress Syndrome. To this day, I can't look at a Military vehicle without getting emotional. In Hudson, we have a reservist building and when I see a person in uniform, I tear up. I see the American Flag, I tear up. I hear the Star Spangled Banner, the same thing happens.

Sometimes when I am alone sitting on my deck, I think of Mike and these 4 years and I am so relieved that he is home safe, I cry. I think I cry more now, than I ever did. I guess I held in those emotions for so long. Just pushed aside my feelings and did what I had to do to get through each day. And when it's finally all over, you can breathe again. And that's when you finally let everything out.

Finally – A firefighter position!

Mike received an email from the government website that he submitted a few of his resumes and applied for many firefighter positions months ago. The letter stated their congratulations and that he was selected for a firefighter position for Westover Air Base which is approximately a little over an hour away. This couldn't have been better timing. Mike I know was hurting somewhat for money as his construction job didn't pay all that well. I had put everything out of my mind for my own sanity. I didn't want to keep worrying and had to start having some faith in God that everything will work itself out.

This position would pay almost three times what he is making now. Mike was on cloud nine. We were so happy for him. Not only a job with health insurance, benefits, vacation and a nice paycheck, but a firefighter position. He was thrilled. He called his friend, Josh. A few weeks later, Josh received a similar e mail offering him a position as well. Not only will he have his good friend with him, but on the same shift.

Eileen Gelsomini

Sometimes I think back to all the worrying I do and how needless it was. Will I ever change and learn. Yes, Val married a nice young man, Yes, Stephanie not only graduated with honors, but was accepted into Grad school and yes, the seemingly impossible happened, Mike became a firefighter. I thank God as I hold my angel stone that gave me strength these last few years. I thank Him for giving me what I prayed for. I have only one unanswered wish – I am still hoping to hold my grandchild in the near future. I know God will answer me.

Our neighbor, John, who entered the Marine Corps with Mike, is now safely home as well. I see him riding in his truck, smiling as he usually does, sporting a beard.

I still sleep fitfully these days, probably leftover residue from my Marine Mom days. I will always be a worrier. But as long as all my children are safe, I will always put my worry into perspective.

I am a better person for this experience. I think back to one Drill Instructor at Parris Island yelling to all of the parents on the tour bus about how they will re-make our children into better people.

How arrogant I thought, the nerve of this man telling us that he will improve upon the job we did.

Hats off to you Drill Instructor. Job well done. Semper Fi

*Footnote: Abigail May Fitzerald – Due September 11, 2009
Born Septermber 21, 2009 7lb 5oz.!

ABOUT THE AUTHOR

Eileen Gelsomini is the mother of three and officially became a "Marine Mom" in 2003.

She writes of her journey through her son's 4 years in the United States Marine Corp. Not knowing any other military family she did not know what to expect.

She kept a journal of what she and her family have experienced from bootcamp and two deployments to Iraq up until her son's discharge.

This story depicts first hand the transformation her son will go through during those 4 years. Her book contains personal unedited emails and letters from her son.

She lives in Massachusetts with her husband and extremely spoiled dog Mia.

Made in the USA
Lexington, KY
26 January 2010